Economic Discrimination Against Women in the United States: Measures and Changes

Economic Discrimination Against Women in the United States

Measures and Changes

Robert Tsuchigane
Frostburg State College

Norton Dodge
University of Maryland

Lexington Books
D.C. Heath and Company
Lexington, Massachusetts
Toronto London

Library of Congress Cataloging in Publication Data

Tsuchigane, Robert.
Economic discrimination against women in the United States.

A revision of R. Tsuchigane's thesis, University of Maryland.
Bibliography: p. 135
1. Woman–Employment–United States. 2. Discrimination in employment–United States.
I. Dodge, Norton T., joint author. II. Title.
HD6095.T77 331.1'33 73-11651
ISBN 0-669-89508-3

Second printing June 1975.

Published simultaneously in Canada.

Printed in the United States of America.

International Standard Book Number: 0-669-89508-3

Library of Congress Catalog Card Number: 73-11651

To our mothers, each of whom has seen the position of women radically changed over more than eight decades

Contents

List of Figures

List of Tables

Preface

This book is primarily a statistical examination of women's earnings and employment based on decennial census and Bureau of Labor Statistics data and other relevant materials. Its purpose is to measure discrimination against women in terms of income, occupation, and participation; to explain factors affecting each type of discrimination; and to separate each type of discrimination into "justified" and "unjustified" components, thereby providing a clearer view of the nature of discrimination and the prospects for reducing or eliminating it.

In analyzing causal factors it is useful to examine not only quantitative factors but also qualitative factors, primarily, legal restrictions and social and cultural conditioning. Our selection of factors affecting each type of discrimination has been influenced by what we consider to be their importance. We have had to be selective. It is impossible in any book on discrimination against women to cover all aspects of the problem.

We are greatly indebted to many federal government officials who were kind enough to provide information. We are particularly indebted to Mrs. Isabelle Streidl who, as chief of the Division of Economic Status and Opportunities, Women's Bureau, U.S. Department of Labor, was of great service in providing relevant information and enlarging our contacts with various agencies of the federal government. Mr. John Buckley, an economist at the Bureau of Labor Statistics, gave us the benefit of his research on earnings differentials between men and women holding the same job. Colleagues, Dr. Kuan I Chen and Dr. Corindo Cipriani gave helpful advice in early stages of the development of this study. Mrs. Jill King was very generous in sharing her firsthand and extensive knowledge of discrimination against women.

We wish to thank Professor Robert E.L. Knight whose comments and suggestions were most helpful in clarifying Chapter 4 and reestimating the demand for women in Chapter 6. We are indebted to Professor Allan G. Gruchy who made valuable comments and suggestions in the early stages of preparing a manuscript. We are also thankful to Professor Lloyd C. Atkinson who made comments on the regression sections of Chapters 4 and 6 and gave us very helpful advice on the interpretation of regression results. We also benefited from discussions of various aspects of discrimination with Sheila Tobias and Alice Rossi, who was kind enough to make a manuscript of her recently published book, *Academic Women on the Move,* available to us. Mary Knight and Homer Dodge provided helpful editorial assistance with parts of the manuscript.

None of the above-mentioned persons is, however, responsible for any of the interpretations that are found in this study. The authors alone are responsible for them.

We are grateful to two computer centers. The computer time for this study was supported in full through the facilities of the computer science centers of the State University of New York at Albany and the University of Maryland.

We would like to express our thanks and to acknowledge permission from the American Anthropological Association to quote from *American Anthropologist* 70: 343, 1968 and from George Allen and Unwin, Ltd. to quote from Michael P. Fogarty et al., *Sex, Career and Family* (1971), p. 505.

Economic Discrimination Against Women in the United States: Measures and Changes

1 Introduction

Sex discrimination persists in our social, cultural, legal, and economic life despite the fact that women can perform equally with men in most occupations provided that there is equal opportunity in training, education, employment, promotion, and pay.

Stimulating the movement for equal rights for women are: (1) the remarkable increase in the participation of women in the labor force; (2) increased approval of women working outside the home; and (3) women's increasing awareness of and restiveness over the denial of equal opportunity in education, employment, promotion, and pay.[1]

A review of the literature on income discrimination indicates that a number of economists have attempted to explain some of the causes and effects of income discrimination in the labor market. Gary Becker, Lester Thurow, James Gwartney, Malcolm Cohen, and most recently Barbara Bergmann, Kenneth Arrow, and Lloyd Atkinson[2] have all measured income differentials between two different racial or sex groups and explained factors affecting productivity and income discrimination.

In her research, Professor Bergmann has developed an integrated concept of income discrimination along the line of marginal productivity theory; she has presented the "crowding hypothesis" that the marginal productivity of blacks and/or women is lowered by the enforced abundance of labor supply in certain occupations because most employers refuse to hire blacks and/or women for jobs in other occupations. Kenneth Arrow, independently of Professor Bergmann, formulated the crowding hypothesis in a similar fashion; he states that when certain jobs are reserved for blacks and other jobs for whites, white wages exceed black wages if the number of blacks in a given occupation is greater than the number of blacks who would otherwise have been in that occupation in the absence of discrimination.

Our approach in Chapter 4 is different from that of Professors Bergmann and Arrow. The marginal productivity of males and females is not estimated in a framework of the production function. Instead, we examine whether net productivity of men is different from that of women in a given occupational group. In analyzing factors affecting net productivity, we determine the difference in output performance between men and women doing the same work and also estimate the difference in nonwage costs between men and women. The economic implications of the legal interpretation of equal pay for equal work are then examined to provide some insights into the extent of income discrimination in the "unjustified" sense.

The crowding hypothesis, though it explains partially the cause of income discrimination as a result of the occupational maldistribution of blacks or women, fails to provide a satisfactory answer in certain professional fields such as law, medicine, science, and engineering which few women enter. It was primarily a group of sociologists[3] that looked into changes in social and cultural conditioning, to provide the kind of analysis necessary to explain the conditions affecting the demand for and supply of women. Economists from Becker to Arrow were, however, interested in the analysis of income discrimination in purely competitive labor and product markets, rather than in the supply of women which is affected by changes in the social and cultural conditioning of women's commitment to work and their attitudes toward certain jobs and careers. Therefore, we consider the adverse effects on the income of women caused by occupational discrimination, the latter being treated in Chapter 5 in the framework of factors affecting the demand for and supply of women in selected occupational groups.

We also consider an integral part of the study to be the analysis of the participation of women in the labor force. The remarkable increase in the labor force participation of women, particularly of married women, has captured the attention of a number of economists who have made detailed analyses. Jacob Mincer, Glen Cain, William Bowen and Thomas Finegan, and Corindo Cipriani[4] have all developed regression equations in an effort to determine the causes of the labor force participation rate of married women. But all have failed to provide the kind of analysis necessary to explain changes in social and cultural conditioning affecting the long-run supply of women, particularly married women. Therefore, some of the demographic, economic, social, and legal factors affecting the participation of women in the labor force are examined in Chapter 6.

Income discrimination, occupational discrimination, and participation discrimination together make up the sum of discrimination which women face. Since the direction and extent of changes in this total are of major interest in formulating social policy and checking its results, we considered it desirable to treat economic discrimination and its components as a whole. Therefore, we begin with a study of economic discrimination and its components, then attempt to explain why changes have occurred, and finally try to separate each type of discrimination into "justified" and "unjustified" components.

We believe that the book provides insights into the extent to which certain factors affecting each type of discrimination can be changed when legal, economic, social, and cultural conditions are changed, and the extent to which others cannot be changed even when these conditions are modified.

Our study begins with an attempt to provide a statistical measure of total discrimination (Chapter 2) and its decomposition into three types of discrimination—income, occupational, and participation (Chapter 3)—and to identify and measure factors affecting each type of discrimination in Chapters 4 through 6.

Chapter 4 analyzes the earnings differential between men and women doing the same work, and separates it on economic grounds into "justified" and "unjustified" components.

Chapter 5 presents a measure of discrimination attributable to social and cultural conditioning and a measure of discrimination in hiring attributable to employers' discriminatory hiring practices. It also separates discrimination in hiring, on the basis of the reasons for nonparticipation, into "justified" and "unjustified" components.

Chapter 6 suggests the importance of the educational attainment and employment opportunity hypothesis in explaining the rise in the participation rate of women in the labor force. It also points out the importance of the favorable attitude of husbands toward wives working outside the home. The final section of the chapter attempts to separate on the basis of reasons for nonparticipation, the difference in the participation rate of men and women into "justified" and "unjustified" components.

And finally, Chapter 7 presents the summary and conclusions of the study and makes some suggestions for further research.

2 Trends in Total Discrimination

Has discrimination against women increased or decreased over the past half century? What kinds of discrimination have increased or decreased? Answers to these questions are crucial to an understanding of the forces which have affected discrimination in the past and the measures which may be taken to change it in the future. To find the answers we must first devise ways to measure changes in total discrimination and then the changes in its components.

Discrimination against women can be defined in a variety of ways. Sometimes it is best to begin with a definition of a certain condition or state by describing the situation which would exist should the condition not be present. Following in this tradition and as a starting point in this study, a rather absolute definition of economic nondiscrimination is employed.

Underlying our definition is the assumption that men and women are equal in their capabilities in almost every respect, provided that women are given the same opportunities for training, employment, and promotion as men. It is also assumed that if men should come to accept equal responsibility for raising the young, caring for the sick or elderly, and looking after the home, the participation of women in the labor force would be essentially equal to that of men. We will also discuss some qualifications to these assumptions of complete equality, due to the physiological differences between men and women. But apart from these qualifications, we assume that men and women, freed of the differentiating effects of social and cultural conditioning, will act and perform in much the same manner.

As an initial point of departure, it is assumed that in the absence of any discrimination women would receive equal pay for equal work, would have essentially the same occupational distribution as men, and would participate in the labor force to the same extent as men. Equality of male and female earnings would be, therefore, the base line against which to measure the degree of discrimination. Departure from this base line (with some exceptions) would indicate that discrimination existed—some justified, some not, some readily removable, some deeply embedded in the social mores of the culture examined. These more tenacious forms of discrimination may take many generations to reduce or to remove completely. We contend, however, that this is the direction that our culture is taking. Even if the reader finds these assumptions difficult to accept or the position and role of women they imply unattractive, he must recognize the usefulness of starting from an extreme but well defined position from which any departures can be readily measured.

This chapter attempts to present a statistical measure of total discrimination against women in the United States economy and its changes over time. We also present and interpret changes in total discrimination and its components for all occupations and for selected occupational groups.

Components of Total Discrimination

Total discrimination, in the sense of the difference between total male and female earnings in the economy, is considered as the sum of three types of discrimination: income discrimination; occupational discrimination; and participation discrimination. Simply stated, to the degree women earn less than men doing the same work, income discrimination exists. Similarly, if the proportion of women in low-paying jobs is larger than in high-paying jobs, occupational discrimination exists. There is still another element of total discrimination based on the difference in the participation of men and women in the labor force. To the extent that the labor force participation rate of women is lower than that of men, participation discrimination exists. We consider this to be the case even if at a certain stage of a society's development more women than men prefer not to work. This might not seem to be a case of discrimination to some. We adhere, nonetheless, to the more absolute view that such departures from identical male and female participation rates are based on social conditioning, which is now changing and should change in the direction of the fuller use of women's capabilities.

Because our measure of total discrimination is the sum of three components which can and may move in different directions, it is important to keep our focus on the three components themselves and upon each of their own movements. For this reason we discuss measures of change over time in income, occupational, and participation discrimination in Chapter 3. At this point, however, it is useful to look at the general problem more closely and at the measure of total discrimination. In symbols total discrimination is written as

$$D_t = \sum_i [(T_m)_i(W_m)_i - (T_w)_i(W_w)_i] \tag{2-1}$$

where $(T_m)_i(T_w)_i$ = the number of full time year-round male (female) workers in the ith occupation;

$(W_m)_i(W_w)_i$ = the median wage or salary income of full fime year-round male (female) workers in the ith occupation.

Equation (2-1)[a] shows that for a condition of "no discrimination" to exist,

[a]Theoretically it would be desirable to compute D_t on the basis of all workers, should earnings and number of workers be adjusted to full time year-round equivalents. The

not only must the earnings of men and women be equal but also the following three conditions must be met simultaneously:

1. Full time year-round female workers earn as much as male workers in the same occupation.
2. Full time year-round female workers are distributed in the same proportion as male workers across all occupations.
3. The number of full time year-round female workers is the same as that of full time year-round male workers for all occupations or in an occupational group.[b]

In reality total discrimination against women is sizable and, instead of the total earnings of women being equal to those of men, the earnings of men are substantially larger. What, then, are the components which make up total discrimination?

Decomposition of Total Discrimination

Consider Example 1 in Table 2-1 which illustrates the decomposition of total discrimination into its three components. Total male (female) earnings are \$220 (\$82) and the difference between total male and female earnings is \$138.

Suppose women are as productive as men doing the same work. Then women should receive the same wage or salary income as men in the same occupation. If such were the case, total female earnings with no income discrimination would be \$97, as shown in Example 2. Therefore, the difference between \$97 and \$82 is attributable to income discrimination. In symbols we write this as

$$D_w = \sum_i (T_w)_i (W_m)_i - (T_w)_i (W_w)_i] \tag{2-2}$$

Consider further that women receive the identical wage or salary income as initially, but are redistributed in the same proportion as men. If such were the case, total female earnings with no occupational discrimination would be \$95, as shown in Example 3. Therefore, the difference between \$95 and \$82 is attributable to occupational discrimination. In symbols we write this as

$$D_0 = \sum_i \left[\left(\frac{T_{mi}}{T_m} \right) T_w (W_w)_i \right] - \sum_i (T_w)_i (W_w)_i \tag{2-3}$$

---

definition of total discrimination employed in this chapter does not, however, preclude the possibility of developing such data when they become available.

[b]We use the 50/50 male-female ratio as a conveniently close approximation to the actual ratio of 48.1 percent men to 51.9 percent women of working age (16 to 65) in 1970.

Table 2-1
Computation of Total Discrimination and Its Components

Example 1

	Men			Women		
Occupation	*No.*	*Earn.*	*Total*	*No.*	*Earn.*	*Total*
1	5	$6	$ 30	10	$5	$50
2	10	7	70	3	6	18
3	15	8	120	2	7	14
	30		$220	15		$82

Example 2

	Men			Women		
Occupation	*No.*	*Earn.*	*Total*	*No.*	*Earn.*	*Total*
1	5	$6	$ 30	10	$6	$60
2	10	7	70	3	7	21
3	15	8	120	2	8	16
	30		$220	15		$97

Example 3

	Men			Women		
Occupation	*No.*	*Earn.*	*Total*	*No.*	*Earn.*	*Total*
1	5	$6	$ 30	(5/30)15	$5	$12.5
2	10	7	70	(10/30)15	6	30.0
3	15	8	120	(15/30)15	7	52.5
	30		$220	15		$95.0

Summary of Examples 1, 2 & 3

Type of Discrimination	*Earnings Differential*
D_t	$138
D_w	15
D_0	13
D_p	110

Finally, consider the case in which both types of discrimination (income and occupational discrimination) are absent. If such were the case, women would receive the same income as men in the same occupation and would be distributed in the same proportion as men. Then total female earnings in the absence of both types of discrimination would be $110. The difference between total male earnings and $110 is attributable to participation discrimination. It is obvious from Example 1 that there are twice as many males participating in the labor force as females. In symbols we write this as

$$D_p = \sum_i (T_m)_i (W_m)_i - \sum_i \left[\left(\frac{T_{mi}}{T_m} \right) T_w (W_m)_i \right] \qquad (2\text{-}4)$$

A summary of the results based on Examples 1, 2, and 3 is found in Table 2-1.

Each of the three measures of discrimination is valid when examined at a given point in time. D_w indicates the proportion of discrimination attributable to income differentials between men and women in total discrimination. Similarly, D_0 shows the proportion of discrimination attributable to the difference in occupational distribution between men and women in total discrimination. Finally, D_p indicates the proportion of discrimination attributable to the difference in the participation of men and women in the labor force.

The value of total discrimination changes over time as each of its components changes. In order to make any measure of discrimination consistent over time it is necessary to have fixed weights in a base year for comparison. Therefore, we are led to the conclusion that income discrimination, occupational discrimination, and participation discrimination require new measures to which Chapter 3 is devoted.[c]

Results

A summary of the results of the application of census data to equations (2-1) through (2-4) for all occupations is presented in Table 2-2.

The census category of all occupations consists of eleven major occupational groups.[d] The availability of income and employment data for the 1940-1970

---

[c]Our measure of income discrimination (D_w), which is based on the assumption that women are as productive as men in each occupation, is a convenient oversimplification. Our measure of occupational discrimination (D_0), which is based on the assumption that women are trained and qualified as equally as men in each occupation, is also a convenient oversimplification. Therefore, the results shown in Table 2-1 should also be interpreted as an approximation. The third element of discrimination, attributable to the difference in the participation of men and women in the labor force, should be interpreted only as an approximation of participation discrimination which is further defined in Chapter 3.

[d]The eleven occupational groups include professional and technical, managerial, farmers and farm managers, sales, clerical, services excluding private household service, operatives, craftsmen, private household service, farm laborers, and laborers excluding farm and mine.

Until 1930 the census followed a procedure of grouping occupations under major industrial groups in which the occupation was usually pursued. In 1940 a pure occupational arrangement was made with occupations grouped in eleven major occupational groups. Since then the census has followed this procedure of grouping occupations under eleven major period enables us to investigate changes in total discrimination in all occupations for this period. Unfortunately, a comparison of total discrimination between 1940 and earlier years is impossible because comparable data are not available.

Table 2-2 shows that the value of the difference between total male and female earnings for all occupations increased from \$226 in 1940 to \$2454 in 1970. The absolute value of D_t, defined as the difference between total male and female earnings, does not indicate whether total discrimination increases, decreases, or remains unchanged.

In order to indicate the degree of change in total discrimination it is necessary to measure D_t divided by total male earnings. Column 3 indicates the extent of total discrimination. When the value of D_t of Column 3 is zero, total female earnings are equal to total male earnings. On the other hand, when the value of D_t of Column 3 is 1.00, total discrimination is at its maximum because total female earnings are zero. Thus, the closer the value of D_t is to unity, the greater the extent of total discrimination. The value of total discrimination is indicated graphically in Figure 2-1 for all occupations, 1940-70. Here each of the three types of discrimination adds up to D_t, as indicated in Column 3 of Table 2-2.

During the 1940-50 period total discrimination decreased by 5 percentage points from .82 to .77. This decline was a result of two opposing forces, participation (occupational) discrimination contributing to a decrease from .68 (.03) to .63 (.02), and income discrimination contributing to an increase from .11 to .12. The significant decrease in participation discrimination was due to the war emergency. When the war was over, many women were forced to leave their high-paying wartime jobs, but nonetheless, more women remained employed in 1950 than in 1940. Also, temporarily, many entered professional and technical employment during the war. Although these women were often forced to take less skilled jobs after the war, the proportion of women in these fields increased from 26 percent in 1940 to 28 percent in 1950.[1] The proportion of women also increased in sales-clerical-service jobs from 22 percent in 1940 to 26 percent in 1950.

In comparison with the 1940-50 period, the 1950-60 period had an increase in total discrimination from .77 to .79. This increase was a result of two forces, income discrimination contributing by an increase from .12 to .13, and occupational discrimination contributing by an increase from .02 to .03. Participation discrimination remained unchanged in the same period.

No period was as significant in reducing the degree of total discrimination as the 1960-70 period, when participation discrimination showed a remarkable decline from .63 to .56. Although income discrimination increased from .13 to .16, occupational discrimination decreased slightly from .03 to .02 during the same period.

---

occupational groups divided into detailed occupations. Not until 1940 did the census offer data for the number of full time year-round workers and the median wage or salary income by sex and occupation.

Table 2-2

Total Discrimination and Its Components for Full Time Year-Round Workers 1940-70[a], and Selected Occupational Groups, 1950-60 and 1960-70 (unit: $100 million)

Occupation	*Type of Discrimination*	*1940* (1)	(2)	(3)	*1950* (1)	(2)	(3)	*1960* (1)	(2)	(3)	*1970* (1)	(2)	(3)
Full Time Year-Round Workers	$(TW)_m$	$275			$589			$1422			$3312		
	D_t	226	100	.82	456	100	.77	1128	100	.79	2454	100	.74
	D_w	30	13	.11	71	16	.12	181	16	.13	534	22	.16
	D_0	8	4	.03	10	2	.02	40	4	.03	76	3	.02
	D_p	188	83	.68	375	82	.63	907	80	.63	1844	75	.56
173 Occupations 1959-60 and 40 Occupations 1960-70	$(TW)_m$				343			752					
	D_t				265	100	.77	596	100	.79			
	D_w				35	13	.10	93	16	.12			
	D_0				61	23	.17	137	23	.18			
	D_p				169	64	.50	366	61	.49			
	$(TW)_m$							2171			3929		
	D_t							1602	100	.73	2603	100	.66
	D_w							393	25	.18	1009	39	.25
	D_0							37	2	.02	69	3	.02
	D_p							1172	73	.53	1525	58	.39

Table 2-2 continued

Occupation	Type of Discrim-ination	1940			1950			1960			1970		
		(1)	*(2)*	*(3)*	*(1)*	*(2)*	*(3)*	*(1)*	*(2)*	*(3)*	*(1)*	*(2)*	*(3)*
Professionals	$(TW)_m$				182			564					
	D_t				135	100	.74	453	100	.79			
	D_w				13	10	.07	36	8	.06			
	D_0				12	9	.07	36	8	.06			
	D_p				110	81	.60	381	84	.67			
	$(TW)_m$							158			331		
	D_t							147	100	.93	285	100	.86
	D_w							30	21	.19	76	26	.23
	D_0							2	1	.03	8	3	.02
	D_p							115	78	.72	201	71	.61
Managers[b]	$(TW)_m$				221			607					
	D_t				205	100	.92	563	100	.92			
	D_w				11	6	.05	32	6	.05			
	D_0				2	1	.01	5	1	.01			
	D_p				192	93	.86	526	93	.86			

White-collar	$(TW)_m$	300			616					
	D_t	131	100	.43	273	100	.44			
	D_w	80	61	.27	216	79	.34			
	D_0	3	3	.01	37	13	.05			
	D_p	48	36	.15	20	8	.05			
	$(TW)_m$				382			594		
	D_t				158	100	.41	333	100	.56
	D_w				133	84	.35	233	70	.39
	D_0				−19	−12	−.05	−16	−5	−.03
	D_p				44	28	.11	116	35	.20
Blue-collar	$(TW)_m$	562			1166					
	D_t	506	100	.90	1062	100	.91			
	D_w	28	5	.05	64	6	.05			
	D_0	5	1	.01	12	1	.01			
	D_p	473	94	.84	986	93	.85			
	$(TW)_m$				1160			2017		
	D_t				987	100	.85	1776	100	.88
	D_w				105	11	.09	146	8	.07
	D_0				195	20	.17	262	14	.13
	D_p				687	69	.59	1368	78	.68

Table 2-2 continued

Occupation	Type of Discrim-ination	1940 (1)	1940 (2)	1940 (3)	1950 (1)	1950 (2)	1950 (3)	1960 (1)	1960 (2)	1960 (3)	1970 (1)	1970 (2)	1970 (3)
Unskilled Workers	$(TW)_m$				396			502					
	D_t				350	100	.88	453	100	.90			
	D_w				20	6	.05	54	12	.10			
	D_0				56	16	.14	82	18	.16			
	D_p				274	78	.69	317	70	.64			
	$(TW)_m$							509			774		
	D_t							447	100	.88	660	100	.85
	D_w							69	15	.14	82	12	.11
	D_0							77	17	.15	77	12	.10
	D_p							301	68	.59	501	76	.64

[a]Includes full time year-round workers for all occupations, excluding farmers, farm managers, and farm laborers.

[b]Data are insufficient for computation in 1960-70.

See text for a full explanation of the notation.

Column 1 indicates dollar value where $(TW)_m$ = total male earnings and total discrimination $D_t = D_w + D_0 + D_p$.

Column 2 shows the proportion of D_w, D_0, and D_p in D_t, by setting D_t equal to 100.

Column 3 indicates the proportion of D_t, D_w, D_0, and D_p in $(TW)_m$, by setting $(TW)_m$ equal to 1.00.

No total discrimination exists if D_t of column 3 is zero. Total discrimination is at its maximum when D_t of column 3 is 1.00.

Source: Bureau of the Census, *1940 Census of Population,* Vol. 3, The Labor Force, Part 1, U.S. Summary, Table 72; *1950 Census of Population,* Vol. 4, Part 1-B, Table 24; *1960 Census of Population,* Vol. 2, Part 7-A, Table 28; *1970 Census of Population,* Vol. 2, Part 8-B, Tables 1 and 7; and *Current Population Report,* P-60, No. 75, Table 49.

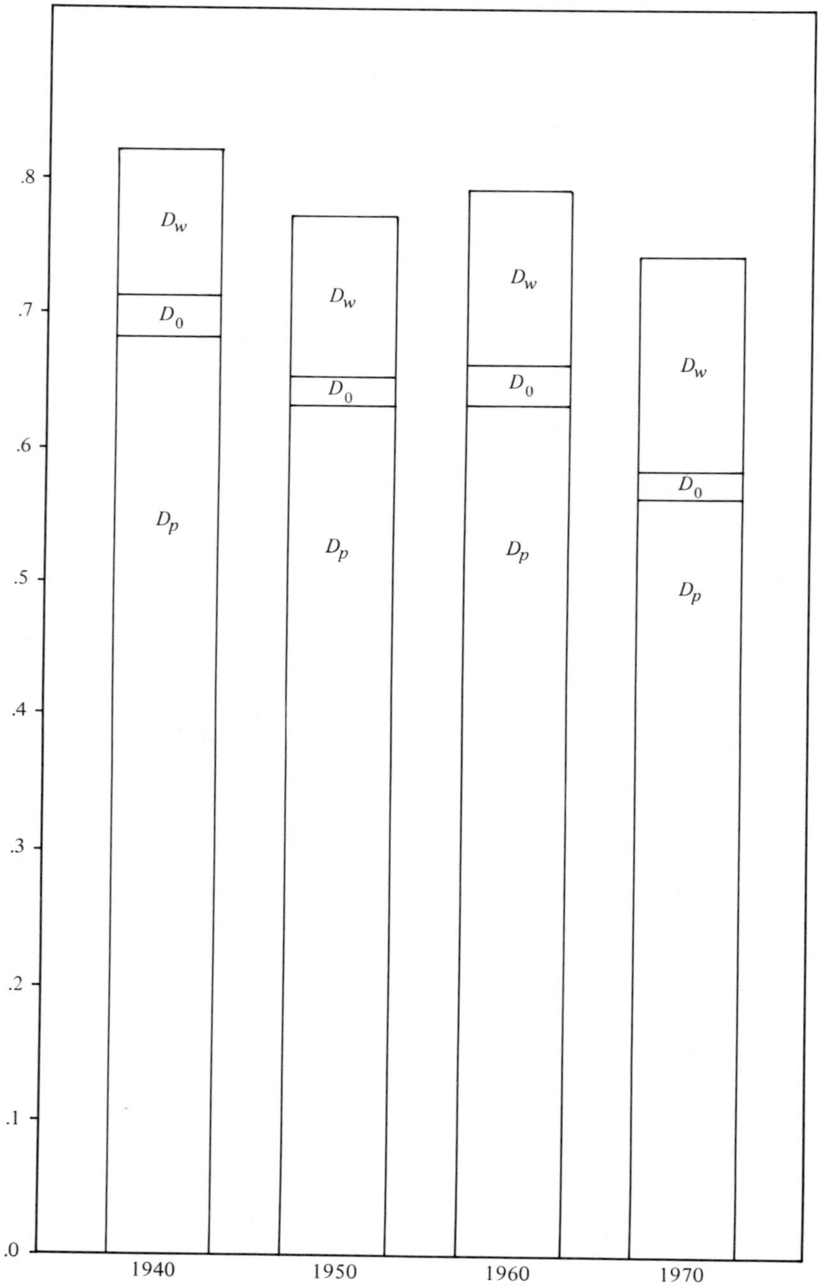

Figure 2-1. Total Discrimination and Its Components for Full Time Year-Round Workers, 1940-70.

Source: Column 3 of Table 2-2.

To obtain more detailed information on total discrimination, 173 occupations were selected which were then subdivided into five occupational groups for comparison. Such disaggregation enables us to compare total discrimination in one occupational group with that in another.

The increase in income discrimination and in occupational discrimination was greater than the decrease in participation discrimination for the 173 occupations during the 1950-60 period. As a result, total discrimination increased from .77 to .79 (Table 2-2).

The situation is different when we look at selected occupational groups. Total discrimination increased from .90 to .91 for the blue-collar group, from .88 to .90 for the unskilled group from .74 to .79 for the professional group, and from .43 to .44 for the white-collar group, while total discrimination remained unchanged for the managerial group in the same period.

Total discrimination was largest (.92) for the managerial group. In contrast total discrimination was the smallest (.43) for the white-collar group. Total discrimination was substantial for the blue-collar and unskilled groups, an area in which a majority of workers are men. Total discrimination for the professional group was in between the male-dominated groups such as the managerial, blue-collar, and unskilled groups and the white-collar group, in which many women were concentrated.

Significant changes in total discrimination and its components for the economy as a whole have occurred over recent decades. Total discrimination decreased from .82 in 1940 to .77 in 1950, primarily due to the impact of World War II. Income discrimination increased, but occupational and participation discrimination decreased in the same period. However, total discrimination increased slightly from .77 in 1950 to .79 in 1960, the period during which both income and occupational discrimination increased whereas participation discrimination remained unchanged. Total discrimination decreased substantially from .79 in 1960 to .74 in 1970, the period during which the Equal Pay Act of 1963 was enacted and sex discrimination in employment was prohibited by Title VII of the Civil Rights Act of 1964. The decrease in total discrimination is attributable to a small decrease in occupational discrimination combined with a substantial decrease in participation discrimination which together were greater than a considerable and rather surprising increase in income discrimination in the same period.[e]

As mentioned earlier, the three measures (D_w, D_0, and D_p) do not have fixed weights in the base year. Therefore, the interpretation of D_w, D_0, and D_p cannot be made with precision. Consequently, new and separate measures of income discrimination, occupational discrimination, and participation discrimination are presented in Chapter 3.

---

[e]A different result may be found on pp. 18-20.

3 Components of Discrimination

While trends and changes in total discrimination in response to various temporary or secular influences are of great interest, the changes that occur in the components of total discrimination are of equal if not greater interest. In assessing the effects of specific developments or policy measures aimed at greater equality, one must focus on one or another of the three specific forms of discrimination to determine how effective a given development or measure has been in producing the observed change.

At the conclusion of our discussion in Chapter 2, we noted that the decomposition of total discrimination into its three components had certain inherent weaknesses. For example, income discrimination is not independent of occupational discrimination. Furthermore, the value of total discrimination computed at a given point in time is not based on fixed weights in the base year for comparison. However, when structural changes in the components of discrimination are marginal or in the same direction, there is no problem in employing the method of measurement presented in Chapter 2. Methods exist, however, which measure changes in one form of discrimination independently of another and avoid all problems of ambiguous or misleading results. These measures take the form of indices for each type of discrimination. They do not and cannot avoid, however, the fundamental index number problem. If the weights employed change significantly over the period of time considered, a Laspeyres-type index will differ from a Paasche-type index, but this was not found to be a serious problem for either of the two indices presented here since the two indices differed by inconsequential amounts in each instance.

Index of Income Discrimination

If the two sexes receive unequal pay for equal work, income discrimination exists. If men and women perform equal work in an occupation, the ratio of women's earnings to men's indicates the degree of income discrimination. A simple average ratio of women's earnings to men's assumes, however, that each occupation is equally weighted. An equally weighted index such as this ignores not only the relative importance of one occupation to another, but also misrepresents structural change in the male-female occupational distribution.

In order to avoid shortcomings inherent in this kind of simple index, an appropriately weighted index of income discrimination is calculated, using weights of occupational distribution for the earlier year. In symbols the index is written as

$$I_w^j = \frac{\sum_i (T_{mi}^{40}/T_m^{40})(W_{mi})^j}{\sum_i (T_{wi}^{40}/T_w^{40})(W_{wi})^j} \quad \text{for } j = 40, 50, 60, \text{ and } 70$$

where $(T_{mi})(T_{wi})$ = the number of full time year-round male (female) workers in the ith occupation;

$(T_m)(T_w)$ = the number of full time year-round male (female) workers in all occupations or in a given occupational group;

$(W_{mi})(W_{wi})$ = the median annual wage or salary income of full time year-round male (female) workers in the ith occupation; and

superscript 40 or j indicates the year 1940 or the jth year.

A change in income discrimination from one period to another is indicated by the index number of income discrimination.[a] Table 3-1 shows that income discrimination for full time year-round workers decreased from 100.0 in 1940 to 97.5 in 1950, largely as a result of the impact of World War II. Many employers in war-related industries paid women almost equal pay for equal work. Few women retained high-paying blue-collar and technical jobs after the war was over. An increase in income discrimination from 97.5 in 1950 to 107.1 in 1960

[a]Consider the following example which contains information on changes in income differentials and in the male-female occupational distribution during two periods.

Example

	Period 1						*Period 2*					
	Men			*Women*			*Men*			*Women*		
Occupation	*No.*	*Earn.*	*T*	*No.*	*Earn.*	*T*	*No.*	*Earn.*	*T*	*No.*	*Earn.*	*T*
1	3	$4	$12	4	$4	$16	5	$6	$30	5	$5	$25
2	4	6	24	1	5	5	6	7	42	3	6	18
3	5	7	35	1	6	6	7	8	56	2	7	14
	12		$71	6		$27	18		$128	10		$57

where T indicates total earnings.

On the basis of this example the index of income discrimination is 1.315 in period 1, indicating that men's earnings were 31.5 percent more than women's. In period 2 the index declined to 1.303, indicating that men's earnings were then 30.3 percent more than women's. For convenience the index of income discrimination is converted by setting I_w in period 1 equal to 100. Results show that income discrimination decreased from 100.0 to 99.1 percent during two periods.

Table 3-1
Income Discrimination for Full Time Year-Round Workers, 1940-70, and Selected Occupational Groups, 1950-60 and 1960-70

Occupation	*1940*	*1950*	*1960*	*1970*
Full Time Year-Round Workers	100.0	97.5	107.1	104.8
	–	100.0	109.8	107.4
173 Selected Occupations	–	100.0	108.7	–
40 Selected Occupations	–	–	100.0	94.4
Professionals	–	100.0	106.1	–
	–	–	100.0	98.2
Managers	–	100.0	103.1	–
	–	–	100.0	98.0
White-collar	–	100.0	107.9	–
	–	–	100.0	99.5
Blue-collar	–	100.0	110.0	–
	–	–	100.0	95.5
Unskilled	–	100.0	122.9	–
	–	–	100.0	104.5

Note: A dash indicates either that no data are available for a certain year or that the data which are available are not compatible with the data in the other year or years compared. The two basic sets of data we use differ in the number of occupations included in each occupational category. Compatible data should become available sometime in 1974.

Source: Bureau of the Census, *1940 Census of Population,* Vol. 3, Part 1, Table 72; *1950 Census of Population,* Vol. 4, Part 1-B, Table 23; *1960 Census of Population,* Vol. 2, Part 1-A, Tables 28 and 29; *1970 Census of Population,* Vol. 2, Part 8-B, Tables 1 & 7.

occurred, followed by a decrease from 107.1 in 1960 to 104.8 in 1970, the period during which the Equal Pay Act was enacted.

Similar results are shown for selected occupational groups. These are professionals, managers, white-collar (clerical, sales, and service workers excluding household service workers), blue-collar (craftsmen and operatives), and unskilled (household service workers and farm and nonfarm laborers) workers. Each of these occupational groups showed a substantial increase in income discrimination from 1950 to 1960.

The increase in income discrimination was 8.7 percent for 173 selected occupations during the 1950-60 period. Among five occupational groups the increase was largest for the unskilled group (22.9 percent) and smallest for the managerial group (3.4 percent). The increases were 10 percent for the blue-collar group, 7.9 percent for the white-collar group, and 6.1 percent for the professional group.

Alleviation of manpower shortages and economic stagnation in the 1950s appear to be among the factors responsible for the increase in income discrimination. These factors are examined in some detail in Chapter 4.

Between 1960 and 1970 there was a slight decrease in income discrimination for full time year-round workers and selected occupational groups, but the level of discrimination still remained above that of 1940. The unskilled group was the only exception in which income discrimination increased between 1960 and 1970.

Index of Occupational Discrimination

The earnings differential between men and women is attributable to differences in wage or salary income and in the male-female occupational distribution. An index of occupational discrimination presented here employs the ratio of total male earnings to total female earnings, using ratios of male wage or salary income to female wage or salary income as weights for the earlier year. If male and female income were kept constant, how would the ratio of total male earnings to total female earnings change when the distribution of males and females changed? In symbols the index of occupational discrimination is written as

$$I_0^j = \frac{\sum_i (T_{mi}^j / T_m^j)(W_{mi})^{40}}{\sum_i (T_{wi}^j / T_w^j)(W_{wi})^{40}} \quad \text{for } j = 40, 50, 60, \text{ and } 70$$

where $(T_{mi})(T_{wi})$ = the number of full time year-round male (female) workers in the ith occupation;

$(T_m)(T_w)$ = the number of full time year-round male (female) workers in all occupations or in a given occupational group;

$(W_{mi})(W_{wi})$ = the median annual wage or salary income of full time year-round male (female) workers in the ith occupation; and

superscript 40 or j indicates the year 1940 or the jth year.

A change in occupational discrimination from one period to another is indicated by the index number of occupational discrimination.[b] Table 3-2 shows occupational discrimination for experienced workers during 1900-1970 and full

[b]Consider the following example which contains information on changes in income differentials and in the male-female occupational distribution during two periods.

time year-round workers 1940-70, indicating that initially a substantial decline occurred for experienced workers from 100.0 in 1900 to 87.2 in 1920, followed by a steady increase from 87.2 in 1920 to 103.1 in 1970. But the situation is different for full time year-round workers. For this more restricted group of workers, occupational discrimination declined sharply from 100.0 in 1940 to 79.7 in 1950, the period during which many women worked in skilled or

Table 3-2
Occupational Discrimination for Experienced Workers, 1900-1970, and Full Time Year-Round Workers, 1940-70

Year	*Experienced Workers*	*Full Time Year-Round Workers*[a]
1900	100.0	na
1910	96.2	na
1920	87.2	na
1930	89.4	na
1940	90.4	100.0
1950	91.2	79.7
1960	95.4	82.0
1970	103.1	86.8

[a]Excludes farmers, farm managers, and farm laborers.

Source: Bureau of the Census, *Occupational Trends in the United States, 1900-1950,* Tables 6a and 6b; *1940 Census of Population,* Vol. 3, Part 1, Table 72; *1950 Census of Population,* Vol. 4, Part 1-B, Table 23; *1960 Census of Population,* Vol. 2, Part 7-A, Table 28; *Current Population Report,* P-60, No. 80, Table 59.

Example

	Period 1						*Period 2*					
	Men			*Women*			*Men*			*Women*		
Occu-pation	*No.*	*Earn.*	*T*	*No.*	*Earn.*	*T*	*No.*	*Earn.*	*T*	*No.*	*Earn.*	*T*
1	3	$5	$15	2	$4	$8	6	$6	$36	4	$5	$20
2	4	6	24	1	5	5	8	7	56	3	6	18
3	5	8	35	1	6	6	6	8	48	3	7	21
	12		$74	6		$19	20		$140	10		$59

where *T* shows total earnings.

On the basis of this example the index of occupational discrimination is 1.298 in period 1, indicating that men's earnings were 29.8 percent more than women's. In period 2 the index went down to 1.225, indicating that men's earnings were 22.45 percent more than women's. For convenience the index of occupational discrimination is converted by setting I_0 in period 1 equal to 100. Results show that occupational discrimination decreased from 100.0 to 94.3 percent during two periods.

technical jobs usually held by men due to World War II. But occupational discrimination increased slightly from 79.7 in 1950 to 82.0 in 1960, the period during which manpower shortages were alleviated. This was followed by a substantial increase in occupational discrimination in the 1960s, the period during which sex discrimination in employment was prohibited by Title VII of the Civil Rights Act. By 1970 the index increased to 86.8.

Similar results are presented in Table 3-3 for selected occupational groups. The table indicates that occupational discrimination for 173 occupations remained almost unchanged from 100.0 in 1950 to 99.9 in 1960. But the situation is different when we look at occupational discrimination in selected occupational groups. Occupational discrimination increased substantially from 100.0 to 122.1 in the professional group, but remained almost unchanged from 100.0 to 99.9 in the managerial group. Discrimination increased slightly from 100.0 to 101.7 in the blue-collar group, but decreased slightly from 100.0 to 93.8 in the white-collar group. In the unskilled group discrimination decreased substantially from 100.0 to 83.6.

Table 3-3
Occupational Discrimination for Selected Occupational Groups, 1950-60 and 1960-70

Occupation	*1950*	*1960*	*1970*
173 Selected Occupations	100.0	99.9	–
	–	–	–
40 Selected Occupations	–	100.0	101.8
Professionals	100.0	122.1	–
	–	100.0	125.4
Managers	100.0	99.9	–
	–	100.0	107.5
White-collar	100.0	93.8	–
	–	100.0	105.5
Blue-collar	100.0	101.7	–
	–	100.0	103.6
Unskilled	100.0	83.6	–
	–	100.0	119.9

Note: A dash indicates either that no data are available for a certain year or that the data which are available are not compatible with the data in the other year or years compared. The two basic sets of data we use differ in the number of occupations included in each occupational category. Compatible data should become available sometime in 1974.

Source: Bureau of the Census, *1950 Census of Population,* Vol. 4, Part 1-B, Table 23; *1960 Census of Population,* Vol. 2, Part 1-A, Tables 28 and 29; *1970 Census of Population,* Vol. 2, Part 8-B, Tables 1 and 7.

Between 1960 and 1970 occupational discrimination for selected groups increased. Increases were largest (25.4 percent) for the professional group and smallest (3.6 percent) for the blue-collar group. Increases were 11.9 percent for the unskilled group, 7.5 percent for the managers, and 5.5 percent for the white-collar group. An examination of some of the factors that caused changes in occupational discrimination in various fields will be found in Chapter 5.

Index of Participation Discrimination

We do not consider a level of participation in the labor force such as 100 percent, to be the proper standard against which to measure the actual participation of women. Rather, we employ the existing rate of labor force participation of men as a norm or standard against which to compare the rate for women. Implicit in the choice of this standard is the assumption that the existing male participation rate for the labor force as a whole represents an upper limit for women. For individual occupations, on the other hand, the number of males engaged may be greater or smaller than the number of women.

The measure of participation discrimination presented here is the number of men employed divided by the number of women employed. A fifty-fifty ratio of men and women in all occupations or in an occupational group implies no participation discrimination or an index of one. If the ratio of men to women is greater than one, participation discrimination against women exists. For example, if women make up only a third of total employment, the index of discrimination would be two. If, on the other hand, the ratio should be less one, participation discrimination against men would exist. Keep in mind, however, that a high proportion of women in an occupational group may be the result of discrimination against women in other occupations, which results in the crowding of women into occupations such as nursing, secretarial work, and other so-called "women's occupations."

Table 3-4 shows participation discrimination, indicating that a continuous decline occurred for experienced workers from 4.46 in 1900 to 1.28 in 1970. A similar pattern of decrease occurred for full time year-round workers from 3.76 in 1940 to 2.26 in 1970. The difference in participation discrimination between experienced (part-time and full time) and full time year-round workers indicates that the proportion of part time women workers is larger than that of part time men workers. The difference was .64 in 1940, but decreased to .16 in 1950, largely due to the impact of World War II. The difference then increased to .61 by 1960, the period during which many women left jobs after the war was over. The difference increased further to .96 in 1970, partly due to women's greater interest in part time work.[1] Despite these differences, the downward trend in participation discrimination shown by both is the overriding matter of interest.

The labor force participation rate of women is lower than that of men for a

Table 3-4

Participation Discrimination for Experienced and Full Time Year-Round Workers and Selected Occupational Groups, 1900-1970 (1.00 = No Participation Discrimination)

Occupational Group	*1900*	*1910*	*1920*	*1930*	*1940*	*1950*	*1960*	*1970*
Experienced Workers	4.46	4.01	3.89	3.53	3.12	2.59	2.05	1.28
Full Time Year-Round Workers[a]	na	na	na	na	3.76	2.75	2.66	2.26
Professionals	1.84	1.42	1.27	1.23	1.41	1.53	1.63	1.38
Managers	21.81	15.41	13.70	11.37	8.10	6.37	5.91	4.52
Farmers	11.51	21.07	22.27	21.92	33.13	35.52	20.51	10.92
Clerical Workers	3.13	1.89	1.10	.93	.85	.61	.48	.30
Sales Workers	4.74	3.63	2.81	3.16	2.73	1.19	1.75	.41
Craftsmen	39.23	39.71	51.70	57.70	45.02	32.06	33.43	21.86
Operatives	1.94	2.20	2.77	3.11	2.88	2.66	2.56	1.94
Household Workers	.03	.04	.04	.05	.06	.05	.04	.03
Service Workers[b]	1.91	1.72	1.71	1.66	1.57	1.24	91	.72
Farm Laborers	6.36	5.00	4.55	5.66	9.66	4.39	4.74	2.64[c]
Laborers (excluding farm and mine)	25.34	41.24	23.69	32.80	35.63	25.72	23.88	14.30

[a]Excludes farmers, farm managers, and farm laborers.

[b]Excludes household service workers.

[c]Preliminary.

Source: Bureau of the Census, *Occupational Trends in the United States, 1900-50,* Tables 6a and 6b; *1940 Census of Population,* Vol. 3, Part 1, Table 72; *1950 Census of Population,* Vol. 4, Part 1-B, Table 23; *1960 Census of Population,* Vol. 2, Part 7-A, Table 28; *Current Population Report,* P-60, No. 80, Table 59.

number of reasons–some physiological and some sociocultural.[c] A one-to-one ratio of men to women in the labor force is, therefore, an ideal which could only be obtained through test tube babies, men taking equal responsibility for the care of children and other household duties (to the extent that these are not institutionalized), and changed attitudes toward women working outside the home at regular jobs.

At the present time, given present attitudes, if women participated in the labor force to the extent of men (79.2 percent), their participation rate would be 36.4 percentage points higher than their present 42.8 percent (see Table 6-3). Of this 36.4 point difference, it is estimated that some 20.9 points are due to sociocultural factors, including the desire not to work, which are embedded to varying degrees in the mores and sociocultural patterns of our society. The burdens and responsiblities of child care account for 12.1 percentage points and 3.0 points are due to the time lost attributable to child birth. Thus, the highest possible proportion of women in the labor force would not be 50 percent (actually 51.9 percent), but 48.9 percent.[d] Given present child care facilities, the realistic percentage for women to aspire to would be 44.5 percent.[e] This is equivalent to a figure for participation discrimination of 1.24[f] which is close to the figure for experienced workers, including part time workers, given in Table 3-4. This suggests that almost as many women are now employed as could be expected, given the present amount of time which has to be devoted to childbearing and child-rearing. This points up the necessity for more child care facilities if more women with young children are expected to enter the labor force.

The experienced and full time year-round worker categories in Table 3-4 are, however, too aggregative to show the interesting changes in participation discrimination in specific occupational groups. To obtain more detailed information on specific participation discrimination, we have also shown major occupational groups in the same table. Participation discrimination in the professional group showed a decline from 1.84 in 1900 to 1.41 in 1940, but increased from 1.41 in 1940 to 1.63 in 1960, followed by a decline from 1.63 in

[c]Physiological differences between men and women and the unique physiological functions of women will be discussed in Chapter 6.

[d]In 1970 labor force participation rates were 79.2 percent for men and 42.8 percent for women. Work time loss due to childbirth was estimated to be equivalent of 3.0 percent of the labor force participation rate (Table 6-4). If women participated in the labor force to the same extent as men, given 3.0 percent work time off, the maximum possible labor force participation rate of women would be 76.2. Based on this figure the proportion of women in the labor force would become 49.0 percent (76.2 divided by the sum of 79.2 and 76.2).

[e]Work time loss due to childbirth and to child care was equivalent of 15.5 percent of the labor force participation rate. The proportion of women in the labor force would be 44.5 percent.

[f]Participation discrimination, using the ratio of 79.2 to 63.7 percent, is 1.24.

1960 to 1.38 in 1970. The professional group did not show much change in participation discrimination between 1900 and 1970, indicating that the proportion of women in the group showed only a mild and gradual change.

Participation discrimination in the managerial field was three to twelve times larger than that in the professional group, ranging from 21.81 in 1900 to 4.52 in 1970. It showed a continuous and substantial decline, however, between 1900 and 1970.

Participation discrimination in the white-collar group also showed a continuous decline during the same period. The clerical occupation, once dominated by men, has become a predominantly female occupation. A shift from men to women gradually took place. In 1970 participation discrimination became .30 compared with the sales occupation (.41) and the service occupation (.72).

Participation discrimination of craftsmen increased from 39.23 in 1900 to 57.70 in 1930, but decreased from 57.70 in 1930 to 21.86 in 1970. Despite a remarkable change in participation discrimination, men still dominated the occupation. Participation discrimination of operatives showed the same pattern of ups and downs as that of the craftsmen during the same period.

Participation discrimination (negative for women) in domestic household service hardly changed between 1900 and 1970, ranging from .03 to .06, though the number of household workers per household decreased sharply during the same period.

Participation discrimination in farm work, as farmers and farm managers, increased from 1900 to 1950 to very high levels, but decreased from 1950 to 1970. Participation discrimination for laborers, excluding farm and mine, had ups and downs between 1900 and 1970, but showed a decline from 25.72 in 1950 to 14.30 in 1970.

As shown in Table 3-4, participation discrimination declined substantially in some occupational groups but only slowly in others such as the professional, farm, blue-collar, service, and unskilled groups. Participation discrimination in private household work virtually remained unchanged between 1900 and 1970.

It is instructive to examine participation discrimination in some selected professional occupations attractive to women. Education, for example, has been the single largest female occupational field. Participation discrimination for elementary and secondary education showed a change from .80 in 1950 to 1.09 in 1960,[2] indicating that men entered the occupation more than women during the 1950-60 period. In higher education participation discrimination decreased from 4.50 in 1960 to 4.44 in 1965,[3] because female instructors increased more than proportionately to their male counterparts. Yet male professors (full, associate, and assistant) increased more than proportionately to their female counterparts during the same period.

Health is another field attractive to women. Female nurses, for example, constitute 85 percent or more of those in the health field. Participation discrimination showed a decline from .43 in 1950 to .17 in 1960[4] because female nurses increased more than proportionately to other male health personnel.

Finally, participation discrimination in federal employment showed a mild decline from 2.05 in 1959 to 1.92 in 1968.[5] This decline was due to increases in nonprofessional female workers, though participation discrimination increased for professional workers.

In summary, a significant decrease in participation discrimination for the economy as a whole occurred between 1900 and 1970. Participation discrimination for experienced workers decreased continuously from 1900 to 1970 and with particular rapidity between 1940 and 1950, reflecting the impact of World War II. It also decreased considerably between 1960 and 1970, the period during which sex discrimination was prohibited by Title VII of the Civil Rights Act of 1964.

Participation discrimination for full time year-round workers showed a similar pattern of decline between 1940 and 1970. The decline was substantial between 1940 and 1950, but only slight between 1950 and 1970.

The data presented on major occupational groups show, in the main, the same pattern of decrease in discrimination decade by decade. The detail given in Table 3-4 permits us to see, however, that the gains for women have been concentrated in certain fields such as clerical and sales work, where gains are a mixed blessing since these are low income occupations; but also, in a smaller way, gains have been made among professionals and managers where pay is high.

A discussion of various factors which are responsible for the increase in the participation of women in the labor force will be found in Chapter 6.

4 Factors Affecting Income Discrimination

In Chapter 1 we saw that Professors Becker, Bergmann, and Arrow followed the traditional marginal productivity approach in their analyses: they assumed purely competitive labor and product markets in attempting to explain why the marginal productivity of blacks is lower and hence their wages are lower than those of whites. In analyzing male-female wage differences, we follow a net productivity approach in an effort to determine the extent to which these differences can be explained by actual differences in net productivity. We also investigate the extent to which they cannot be explained, but are due to discrimination in an "unjustified" sense. Therefore, in analyzing factors affecting the difference in earnings between men and women doing the same work, it is necessary to determine differences in their net productivity. Toward this end, differences in both productive performance and in nonwage costs of men and women in selected occupational groups are measured. Differences in earnings of men and women are then decomposed on economic grounds into components attributable to differences in hours worked, educational attainment, job seniority, and absenteeism. There is also a residual due to other factors some of which can be identified but not individually measured.[a]

The overly broad census definition of occupation makes it impossible to determine precisely the extent to which the unexplained component is due to income discrimination in an "unjustified" sense. Therefore, the economic implications of a number of court decisions on equal pay for equal work are examined to determine whether one might reduce or eliminate these "unjustified" differences in earnings. The final section of the chapter attempts, on the basis of these various findings, to separate on economic grounds the difference in earnings between men and women into "justified" and "unjustified" components.

[a]Richard B. Mancke in his article on "Lower Pay of Women: A Case of Economic Discrimination," in *Industrial Relations,* Vol. 10 (October, 1971) argues that the earnings differential between men and women attributable to differences in job seniority, labor turnover, and labor productivity should be taken into account in an attempt to evaluate whether women are discriminated against in wages and salaries. Larry E. Suter and Herman P. Miller in their article on "Income Differences Between Men and Women," in *American Journal of Sociology,* Vol. 78 (January, 1973), decompose earnings differentials between men and women 30 to 44 years old on the basis of differences in education, occupational status, hours worked, lifetime career experience, plus a residual. Among the five components the unexplained residual was the largest, followed by lifetime career experience and then hours worked. Education and occupational status was relatively small in explaining the earnings differential of men and women.

The net productivity approach we follow assumes that men and women in the same job category are substantially equal in performance or output, i.e., labor productivity. In our examination we would like to investigate all occupational groups. However, few detailed and reliable studies have been made which are useful for our purposes. In many occupations, particularly service occupations, a major problem is measuring output or production on a comparable basis. In simple office or machine-assisted factory production work, however, it is not difficult to measure performance or output by sex under similar working conditions. Some reliance may be placed, therefore, on two studies by the Bureau of Labor Statistics: one on labor productivity in office work and the other in production work in the footwear and furniture industries. These studies show that the productivity of men and women on the average differed by less than five percentage points.[1] Unfortunately, comparable studies on productivity for executive, administrative, and professional personnel by sex and field are lacking, which makes it difficult to determine whether women are as productive as their male counterparts in these fields. Despite this, there is one area in which scholarly productivity by sex and field can be measured with some simplicity and some degree of reliability. This is productivity in professional or scholarly publication.

Differences in Scholarly Productivity between Male and Female Professionals

Previous studies of scholarly productivity have often failed to provide a meaningful index of productivity.[b] They may have lacked a sufficient number of

---

[b]Professors Dykman and Stalnaker, "Survey of Women Physicians Graduating from Medical School, 1925-1940," in *Journal of Medical Education,* Vol. 32, Table 29, have made the first comprehensive survey of the scientific productivity of men and women physicians who took their medical degrees between 1925 and 1940. This survey shows that women physicians were as productive as their male counterparts when the number of articles published was less than ten. But when the number of articles published was ten or more, women physicians were about one half as productive as men physicians.

Ann Fisher and Peggy Golds, "The Position of Women in Anthropology," in *American Anthropologist,* Vol. 70 (April, 1968), p. 343, state that "there is no objective evidence of discrimination against women when judging by their rate of publication in the *American Anthropologist.*" Apparently what they intended to say is that women anthropologists are as productive as their male counterparts in publication. Indeed the percentage of women in the profession was 17.6 in 1968 and the percentage of articles by women in the *American Anthropologist* in 1967-68 was 16.2 (6 of 37 articles authored by women), the ratio of the latter to the former being .92.

However, an examination of articles from three leading journals in anthropology, namely, *American Anthropologist, American Journal of Physical Anthropology,* and *Southwestern Journal of Anthropology* during the five year period between 1966 and 1970 indicates that women were more productive in 1970 and 1968 than in 1966, 1967, and 1969. Thus, the statement by Fisher and Golds is biased because they have selected only one journal in which women were highly productive in 1967-68. See Table 4-1 for the results of a more significant sample of 650 articles in anthropology.

observations; they may have been based on responses to questionnaires which say nothing of the nature or quality of the publication; they may have used the wrong universe in determining the proportion of potential male and female contributors, and so forth. We shall not limit our measure of productivity to college and university professors,[c] but will include qualified professionals of all types—researchers in industry and government—by field and sex.

In an effort to improve upon these studies, much larger samples of articles (largest: 9,485 and smallest: 559) in twenty major scholarly fields were employed here to determine the percentage of articles published by women in each specialty. The percentage of articles was then compared to the percentage of women in that field or specialty, to determine if their scholarly productivity was a large as might be expected were they as productive as men.

There are several problems which render this approach less precise than desirable, but efforts have been made to overcome them.

First, the proportion of articles by men and women cannot be determined with certainty due to the frequent use of initials instead of first names, but when such cases are eliminated, a large and represenatative sample still remains.

Second, selection of the proper universe for the determination of the percentage of women who might publish in a field is critical. For example, considering the field of mathematics, the question of whether persons teaching mathematics in high schools be included in the universe arises. If so, the proportion of women in the field would be much larger than if only university professors of mathematics were included. Perhaps the latter is the proper universe. To resolve this question we have used the National Science Foundation data on "qualified scientists" for fifteen fields, and the Bureau of Labor Statistics estimate of "women Professionals" for the remaining five fields in our analysis.

Third, the selection of journals both from the standpoint of their importance in a field and their representativeness of the various specialties within that field is essential to provide a meaningful and representative sample of articles for each field. An effort was made with the advice of both librarians and professionals to select the most significant and representative journals in each field and to make each sample at least as large as 500 articles (see Appendix A). In only four of the twenty fields was the sample smaller than 750 articles.

Results

Table 4-1 shows that among the natural sciences and engineering, women's scholarly productivity as measured by publication of journal articles is much lower than that of men. It is highest in chemistry (.63), followed by biological

---

[c]The performance of male and female professors in principle may be evaluated based on several criteria which include: (1) mastery of subject matter; (2) effectiveness in teaching; (3) publication of articles and books; and (4) quality of publication. Research grants and

sciences (.40), computer science (.21), and earth sciences (.16). In mathematics and statistics women's productivity is substantially low (.11 and .09 respectively). Engineering is a field in which women's productivity (.10) lies between

Table 4-1
Percentage of Women in Various Specialities Compared with Percentage of Articles in Related Professional Journals Contributed by Women, 1970

Field	*Percentage of Women in Speciality (1)*[a]	*Percentage of Articles by Women (2)*[b]	*Ratio (2)/(1) (3)*	*Sample Size (4)*
Natural Science				
Mathematics	11	1.3	.11	5,140
Statistics	11	1.0	.09	1,455
Computer Science	10	2.1	.21	559
Physics	4	.3	.07	1,001
Atmospheric Sciences	2	.2	.10	800
Earth Sciences	3	.5	.16	1,882
Chemistry	7	4.4	.63	924
Biological Sciences	13	5.2	.40	758
Engineering	1	.1	.10	930
Social Science				
Anthropology	19	8.1	.44	650
Economics	6	1.7	.28	638
Political Science	10	4.4	.44	1,125
Psychology	24	9.3	.38	9,485
Sociology	12	5.6	.47	5,761
Humanities				
English	50	6.5	.13	9,105
Plays (Theater)	50	12.6	.25	4,179
History (U.S.)	10	1.5	.15	2,048
Linguistics	23	2.7	.12	7,693
Education	25	7.6	.30	1,649
Law	4	.2	.05	668

[a]Derived from *National Register of Scientific and Technical Personnel 1970,* Table A-59 and *College Education Workers 1968-80.*

[b]For the selection of professional journals and method of making article counts see Appendix A.

Sources: National Science Foundation, *National Register of Scientific and Technical Personnel 1970,* Table A-59; Bureau of Labor Statistics, *College Education Workers 1968-80* (Bulletin 1676, 1970); and Selected professional journals in each specialty.

---

professional awards and recognition within or ouside the university would provide another performance criterion. Among these criteria only publication is a readily quantifiable measure of performance. While recognizing its limitations in practice, most studies have used some index of publication as a measure of scholarly productivity of men and women.

mathematics and statistics, while physics is a field in which women published least in relation to what should be expected (.07).

In the social sciences women appear to be relatively more productive, but still less than half as productive as men. In descending order by field, women contributed to sociology (.47), anthropology (.44), political science (.44), psychology (.38), and economics (.28).

In the humanities women are more productive in the authorship of plays and other literature (.38) than in history (.15) and linguistics (.12), but again they are far less productive than men in literary output.

Women's productivity in the literature of higher education (.30) is less than that in chemistry, biological sciences, anthropology, political science, psychology, and plays and literature. Women published more articles in journals of elementary education than in journals of secondary and higher education or educational administration.

Women are least productive relative to men in the field of law where the ratio is only .05, lower than in engineering or any field in the natural sciences, social sciences, humanities, and education.

Reasons for Lower Scholarly Productivity

With respect to academic productivity, Jessie Bernard in her book *Academic Women* suggests that the productivity index would be more meaningful should women have rank, tenure, salary, and other professional privileges and benefits similar to those of men.[2] Unfortunately, data necessary for measuring productivity under substantially similar conditions for men and women are not available. Therefore, our index may underestimate to a degree the productivity of women in publication.

A number of other factors may help explain why women in each field are less productive than men. In a survey of personal and environmental factors affecting the productivity of women, Helen Astin points out that one of the most significant determinants is the quality of the doctorate-granting institution. She states that most of the differences in productivity are attributable to institutional affiliation (college vs. university), since university-employed professors are more productive than college-employed ones without regard to sex. The productivity of women trained or teaching in leading universities is closer to that of males than that of academic women as a whole.

Apart from differences between men and women in environment (college vs. university) and the proper role in higher education (scholar vs. educator), there are sex differences in productivity which may be attributable to childbearing and child-rearing, career motivation, special problems of social adjustment, and different interests and abilities. These will be discussed in turn.

1. Time and momentum lost due to career interruption, childbearing and

child-rearing may have an important effect on scholarly productivity. Married women have more family responsibilities than their male counterparts, and do more household chores. The availability of domestic service or child care facilities may help lighten the burden of household work to some extent, but the presence of a young child requires much attention.

2. Women may have a different professional career motivation. In most cases men will be devoted to their speciality, while married women, with or without children, have dual commitments—conscientious roles as wife and mother and professional careers ouside the home. Many married women resolve their dual involvements with their husbands' cooperation and support. But married women who do not get this kind of cooperation and support find their career motivation seriously, if not entirely, weakened.

3. Single professional women have a special problem of adjustment in the male-dominated community. They often feel themselves outsiders in the social sense; their interests are not the same as those of married women in the community, nor are their interests the same as those of their male colleagues. The Radcliffe study of single professional women revealed that these kinds of specific problems would reduce women's productive enthusiasm and efficiency.[3]

4. Men and women have different interests and abilities according to a number of responsible studies.[d] Such differences in interests and abilities may affect the development of publication potential. Our findings show that women are more productive in the fields of biology and chemistry than in physics. They also published more in the humanities, the arts, and psychology than in economics and political science. Our findings also support the view that women have different abilities to cope with certain types of abstract or complex problems, even though both men and women have equal educational backgrounds and other qualifications.[e]

In conclusion, although the productivity of women in office or factory work is substantially the same as that of men, there is less conclusive evidence that

---

[d]There exist well-established differences in the interests and attitudes between men and women in Western cultures. Parson and Bales describe such differences in *Family, Socialization, and Interaction Process,* London: Routledge and Kagan Paul, 1956, p. 149.

Sex differences between men and women in verbal ability, quantitative ability, spacial conceptualization, and creative and imaginative ability are well documented. Some explanations are more acceptable than others. Social and cultural explanations are more acceptable than genetic and biological ones. If they are social and cultural, they can be more readily reduced or eliminated, if women were in the same social and cultural environment in all possible stages of human development. But the situation is more complicated than the logic suggests because the relation between biological and social and cultural factors may be complex. Thus, the central issue appears to be to what extent such differences in interests and abilities may affect the productivity of women.

[e]In chemistry, for example, three leading journals were examined. *Journal of Inorganic and Nuclear Chemistry* and *Journal of Physiology* contained more theoretical articles than *Microchemical Journal.* Women published 26 articles in *Microchemical Journal* (26 of 246) while they contributed 15 of 678 articles to the two other journals.

women in business and executive positions are as productive as men. In scholarly productivity, women appear to be less productive, even if the results are corrected for underestimation. As initially indicated, women's lower productivity is partially attributable to discrimination against women and partially to the time and momentum lost due to career interruption. If women and men were in similar professional environments, women's productivity might be more similar to that of men. For more insight into the reasons for differences in the earnings of women, we must look further and examine factors other than productivity *per se.*

Differential Earnings between Men and Women Attributable to Differences in Selected Variables and Other Factors

Using a sample in the Florida area, James Gwartney[4] estimated the income differential between male whites and male nonwhites in 1965. He employed the ratio of the median income of nonwhites to white males, under the assumption that nonwhite (or white) males were distributed among productivity categories as white (or nonwhite) males. The income differential was then decomposed into a part attributable to differences in productivity factors,[f] and a residual unexplained by differences in productivity factors.

Gwartney's approach seems valid for determining the effect of each of the selected productivity factors on the earnings differential between white and nonwhite males. It also enables one to determine the cumulative effect of each selected productivity factor on the earnings differential between white and nonwhite males, provided that classification tables involving two or more variables are available. As a result, Gwartney's method offers promise in studying the effect of various productivity factors on the earnings differential between men and women.

However, since the national data on Gwartney's productivity factors are lacking for 1950, 1960, and 1970, it is impossible to determine the effect of each productivity factor on the earnings differential between men and women, using Gwartney's method for the years for which we have census data on income differentials. Among productivity factors affecting the earnings differential between men and women doing the same work, we shall consider the following four factors for which we do have data. They are: (1) hours worked; (2) educational attainment; (3) job seniority; and (4) absenteeism. No further explanation of the difference can be made due to the absence of information on

[f]The productivity factors employed were quantity of education, scholastic achievement, state distribution, city size, and age distribution. Locational factors such as state distribution and city size are not generally considered as productivity factors, but they were included because they affect the earnings capacity of workers. Age distribution was also included for the same reason.

other factors which might include nonwage costs such as turnover, cost of child care, and abandoned careers. Locational factors included in the Gwartney study are not considered here, on the assumption that locational factors may not significantly affect the earnings differential between men and women doing the same work in a similar location. It is rather the type or size of establishment that affects the earnings differential.[5]

The four explained causes for differences in male and female earnings were calculated as follows:

Hours Worked

Since decennial census data on year-round workers (50-52 weeks) include both full time and part time year-round workers, it is necessary either to obtain earnings of full time year-round workers by sex, or to compute additional earnings that female workers would have earned had they worked to the same extent as their male counterparts.[g] Following the latter method, we find that women in all occupations for 1970 would have earned $575 more than they actually did had they worked 4.72 weeks longer than their actual work time.[h] Additional earnings were largest ($824) for professionals and smallest (–$7) for laborers, excluding farm and mine laborers.

Educational Attainment

Educational attainment is intended to measure the level of capability for all types of jobs as a proxy of productivity. A person with more education is assumed to be more productive than a person with less education. We asked how much more women of equivalent education would have earned had they been distributed in the same education-occupation group as their male counterparts.

In 1970, for example, women in all occupations would have earned $360 more than they actually did. Such earnings were largest ($641) for managers and smallest for farm laborers (–$34). Because of the unavailability of data required to make similar computations for 1960 and 1950, it was necessary to employ the less desirable regression method to estimate the effect of education on the earnings differential between men and women. The regression coefficients were found to be significant for each occupational group by sex.

---

[g]The variable, hours worked, is a preferred measure over that of weeks worked.

[h]Census data on hours worked in 1970 were not available at the time of writing, so we employed BLS data on weeks worked by sex. Men worked 44.53 weeks compared with 39.81 weeks for women. The difference was 4.72 weeks. The additional earnings women would have earned had they worked 4.72 weeks longer were calculated on the basis of (4.72/39.81) multiplied by $4873, i.e., $575 where $4873 are earnings of full time year-round female workers in all occupations.

We asked what the earnings differential would be if the regression coefficient of education for women were set equal to that of education for men. In 1960 the earnings differential between men and women attributable to the difference in educational attainment was $16 for 173 occupations.[i] The difference was largest ($151) for the managers and smallest (–$425) for the unskilled group, where the regression coefficient was larger for women than for men. The differences were $15 for the professional group, –$12 for the blue-collar group, and –$91 for the white-collar group. Similar results were also obtained for 1950.

As will be seen in column 5 of Table 4-2, the difference in the value of education between 1960 and 1970 is attributable to the difference in male-female occupational distribution. Women of equivalent educational attainment are concentrated in low-paying jobs within an occupation. Large differences are more pronounced for professionals, managers, and sales persons. Small differences exist for craftsmen and clerical and service workers, indicating that occupational distribution by sex changed little between 1960 and 1970. Negative values of education for farm and nonfarm laborers show that educational attainment was higher for women than for men.

Job Seniority

Job seniority[6] is intended to measure the length of work experience as a proxy of productivity. A person with longer work experience is assumed to be more productive than a person with shorter work experience. If such is the case, higher pay based on longer service reflects higher productivity. For example, most manufacturing firms use pay schedules graduated by length of service for workers under union contract, but not for all employees. Many nonmanufacturing companies also have pay schedules graduated by length of service. In professional and managerial occupations, job seniority is still considered to be very important, since these occupations involve long-range career training after an applicant has met the educational requirements and qualifications.[7]

Bureau of Labor Statistics data on job seniority were used to compute the additional earnings that female workers would have had if they stayed on the job as long as their male counterparts. Such additional earnings were calculated on the assumption that a compound rate of growth of three percent occurred.[j] If

[i]The male regression coefficient of E is 3.35 and the difference in E between men and women is (11.96 – 11.91) years. Thus, 3.35 times .05 = .1625 which indicates $16.25 in the regression equation we employed.

[j]The rate of increase in wage and salary income of full time year-round workers differs from one occupational group to another. Such rates of annual increase during the 1965–70 period, for example, were the largest (7.3 percent) for the professionals and the smallest for the craftsmen (5.9 percent). However, these rates of increase include increases in pay and in promotion. In the absence of data on the rate of increase attributable to job seniority, we employed a three percent rate of increase, which reflects the historical economic growth rate in real terms, substituted for the rate of increase in job seniority.

Table 4-2
Earnings Differential Between Men and Women Attributable to Differences in Selected Variables and to Other Factors for All and Selected Occupational Groups, 1950-70

		Earnings			*Difference Due to*					
Occupational Group	*Year*	*Male (1)*	*Female (2)*	*Diff. (3)*	*Hours Worked (4)*	*Educa-tion (5)*	*Job Sen-iority (6)*	*Absen-teeism (7)*	*Unexplained Residual (8)*	*Percentage Unexplained (9)*
All Occupations	50	$3110	$1997	$1113	$238	$ 35	$ 94	–	$ 746	67.0
	60	5354	3161	2193	651	16	262	$ 4	1260	57.4
	70	9030	4873	4157	575	360	360	8	2854	68.7
Professionals	50	4030	2600	1430	288	7	143	–	992	69.3
	60	6841	4209	2632	947	15	218	12	1440	54.7
	70	12237	7172	5065	824	443	394	16	3398	67.1
Managers	50	4327	2536	1791	265	49	84	–	1393	77.7
	60	7208	4119	3089	506	151	329	5	2098	67.9
	70	12101	6246	5855	537	641	324	32	4321	73.8
Sales Workers	50	3136	2235	901	116	43	94	-	648	71.9
	60	5446	3737	1709	153	80	265	9	1202	70.3
	70	8536	5366	3170	445	144	364	0	2217	69.9
Clerical Workers	50	3270	1632	1638	293	42	5	–	1298	79.2
	60	5541	2309	3232	701	91	42	27	2371	73.4
	70	10093	3809	6284	312	486	159	22	5305	84.4
Craftsmen	50	3378	2265	1113	238	65	6	–	804	72.2
	60	5727	3592	2135	387	10	229	–29	1538	72.0
	70	9034	5370	3664	628	55	64	– 4	2921	79.7

Operatives	50	2924	1920	1004	108	56	48	–	792	78.8
	60	4886	2924	1962	412	15	87	3	1445	73.6
	70	7863	4432	3431	589	30	53	1	2758	80.3
Service Workers	50	2425	1402	1023	148	45	73	–	757	73.9
	60	3953	2081	1872	381	95	126	5	1265	67.5
	70	6857	3666	3191	590	52	143	12	2394	75.0
Laborers Excluding Farm and Mine	50	2366	1900	466	166	–280	–	–	580	–25.7
	60	4016	2885	1131	190	–400	–	–	1341	–18.5
	70	6446	4170	2476	– 7	– 31	– 87	3	2598	– 4.9
Farm Laborers	50	1228	656	572	354	–270	–177	–	665	–16.2
	60	1977	901	1076	207	–450	– 25	1	1343	–24.8
	70	4147	2595	1552	65	– 34	–609	0	2130	–37.2

Columns 1 and 2: Bureau of the Census, *1950 Census of Population,* Vol. 4, Part 1-B, Table 23 (50 PC(4)1B,23 for short); *1960 Census of Population,* Vol. 2, Part 7-A, Tables 28 and 29 (60 PC(2)7A, 28-29 for short); and *1970 Census of Population,* Vol. 2, Part 8-B, Tables 1 and 7 (70 PC(2)8B, 1-2 for short).

Column 4: Bureau of the Census, 50 PC(4)1B,14; 60PC(2)7A,13; Bureau of Labor Statistics, *Special Labor Force Report* No. 141, Table A-4 (SPFR 141, A-4 for short).

Column 5: Bureau of the Census, 50 PC(4)1B, 10 and 60 PC(2)7A,9.

Column 6: Bureau of Labor Statistics, *Current Population Report* P-50, No. 36, Table 4; SLFR 77, F; and SLFR 112, F.

Column 7: Department of Health, Education and Welfare, Public Health Service, *Selected Characteristics by Occupation: United States July 1961-June 1963,* p. 40; and *Time Lost from Work Among the Currently Employed Population, United States 1968,* Table 9 (1972).

the difference in the median years of job seniority between men and women is positive as in most cases, women should have earned at the rate of $(1.03)^t$, where t is the difference in years of job seniority.

In 1970, for example, women in all occupations would have earned \$360 more than they actually did, had they stayed on the job for 2.7 years longer than their male counterparts. Additional earnings attributable to the difference in job seniority were the largest (\$394) for professionals and the smallest (–\$609) for farm laborers. The same computation was made for 1960. Results by major occupational group are shown in column 6 of Table 4-2.

Absenteeism

Absenteeism costs the employer money through loss of production, through forced substitution of workers in jobs for which they may not be fully trained, and through additional cost of training replacements or stand-by employees. Absenteeism costs workers money through reduced earnings, but this is not our present concern.

Job absence may be attributed to health and nonhealth reasons. The Bureau of Labor Statistics, in its monthly survey of the labor force, records the number of persons absent in the entire nonagricultural economy[k] due to illness,[l] vacations, and other reasons, but the duration of each kind of absence is not given. Because of this, it is impossible to compute the work-loss days by reason. Therefore, we must make use of two surveys which provide the necessary kind of information for 1960 and 1970. According to the latter survey,[m] women were absent from work due to illness more than men (5.6 versus 5.2 days), a difference of only 0.4 day per year.

The maximum possible cost to the employer of female absenteeism due to sickness is defined as the excess of female over male work loss days multiplied by the average daily earnings of women. In 1970, for example, the extra cost of female absenteeism for all occupations was only \$8.00. This very small figure

[k] The Bureau of Labor Statistics defines the absentee rate as the ratio of the number of man-days lost through job absence to the average number of employees times the number of scheduled working days. Thus, if the local telephone company employs 300 employees on the average and 200 man-days are lost through job absence during one month, that is, 22 working days, the absentee rate is:

$$\frac{200}{300 \times 22} \times 100 = 3.03 \text{ percent.}$$

[l] Illness includes both sickness and accidental injury, occupational and nonoccupational, and absences due to other health reasons.

[m] The sample size of the survey was 38,000 households. The survey included each of major geographic regions and urban and rural sectors of the United States, representing the 1960 population by sex, race, and residence.

indicates that absenteeism of women can in no way justify wage or salary differentials between men and women as a whole. Even in specific occupational groups such as managers, the differential due to absenteeism is small ($32.00).

A number of other factors affecting the male-female earnings differential are difficult to measure. Therefore, we merely take brief note of several of them. These include: (1) the cost of labor turnover to the employer; (2) the cost of child care; and (3) the cost of career abandonment. These three factors will be discussed below.

Rate of Separations

Labor turnover costs the employer through the additional hiring and training of employees. Women customarily quit jobs more frequently than men. Their rate of separations per month was 2.4 per 100 compared with 1.8 per month per 100 male workers in the 1950-1955 period.[8] The average monthly separation rates for women and men factory workers in 1968 were 2.6 and 2.2 respectively.[9]

In an attempt to evaluate the economic implications of male and female labor turnover among professionals, John Parrish made a survey of men and women chemists in 65 industrial laboratories.[10] Sixty-five percent of the laboratories surveyed indicated that average turnover rates were higher for women than for men. But the overall average rates are misleading because chemists at the lower level had higher turnover rates than those at the higher level. When chemists were grouped by academic degree, women's turnover rates were about the same as men's. Less than ten percent of the laboratories reported that women's turnover rates were much higher. About ninety percent of the laboratories reported that women's turnover rates were equal to or slightly higher than men's.

The cost to an employer of an employee quitting will vary with the amount the employer invests in his employees. Hiring costs and training costs are positively related to the skill level or earnings of employees and inversely to their turnover rates.[11] The American Management Association estimated that the average turnover cost per worker in 1960 was $500,[12] but varied with skill and occupation. For example, a file clerk may cost the employer $300, but a highly trained engineer may cost an employer $10,000 or more.

Cost of Child Care

If an employer supplies partially or fully subsidized child care facilities, their operation becomes an additional cost to the employer of employing women entering or in the childbearing and child-rearing age group. Since child care facilities are not yet provided by employers on a large scale basis, estimates of costs to employers are scarce and not necessarily representative or meaningful.

A conservative estimate by the Women's Bureau of the total capital outlay for constructing or renovating a day care center was approximately $2,000 per child.[13] Operating costs vary considerably, depending upon the type of care and the area being served. The Women's Bureau reports that operating costs range from $400 to $750 or more per child.[14] The Head Start experience indicates, however, that the average annual cost per child between three and five years of age ranges from $1,245 to $1,862.[15]

Although there is increased interest by employers in the provision of child care facilities, they have preferred for the most part to avoid bearing these costs themselves.[16] Eight of the nine companies surveyed subsidized 20 to 50 percent of the operating cost, the remaining 50 to 80 percent of the cost being charged to users of the day care facilities. Only one company subsidized the entire operating cost. Rather than an increase in employer-provided facilities, an increase in government provided or subsidized facilities would appear likely in the future. Accordingly, we may conclude that for the future the possible cost of child care facilities is not a likely deterrent to most employers in deciding whether to employ a man or a woman or in justifying differences in pay.

Since employers do not seem likely to provide adequate child care facilities under any circumstances, it would be desirable in the interests of justice and equality for the facilities to be provided by the state, just as elementary and secondary education are provided today. Children should be, in the language of economists, the joint product of men and women. Viewed in this light, there can be no justification for leaving the burden of child care on women alone. Therefore, in the longer run, with the adequate provision of child care facilities, their cost should in no way be a factor which an employer would consider when deciding whether or not to employ women.

Cost of Career Abandonment

Abandoned careers is another cost to society which appears to be higher for women than for men. In the absence of data with a broad coverage, it is impossible to arrive at a conclusive answer to the question of male-female differences in abandonment. It is instructive, however, to look at a major survey of the attrition rate of male and female medical students as an example of the problem.

This survey was based on a 10 percent sample of 71,140 male and 4,713 female medical students during the period 1949-58. The 10 percent sample was representative of the student body as a whole, because it was selected from 28 representative medical colleges in different geographic regions and from among students of different ability levels.

This survey shows that the attrition rate attributable to academic reasons was 7.3 percent for women and 4.9 percent for men.[17] But when we look at the attrition rate attributable to nonacademic reasons, we find that the rate was 8.2

percent for women compared with 3.3 percent for men.[18] This higher attrition rate for women is an additional cost to society because it reduces the net productivity of women versus men. Thus, there is some economic justification for applying higher admission standards for women to medical school.[n] These higher rates reflect in part, however, a failure to adjust medical working conditions to the needs of women. With some adjustment in working conditions and an improvement in attitudes toward women physicians, career abandonment rates might be reduced to levels very close to those of men.

Thus, we may conclude that the difference in the attrition rate between men and women medical students might be reduced to a marginal level, perhaps to less than a few percentage points, if medical schools made special provisions for women's unique problems: pregnancy, childbirth, care of children, etc. Failure to make these adjustments could cost society more through the loss of the productive services of women who abandon careers than the improvements in working conditions would cost.

This example from medicine clearly suggests that the excess of female over male career abandonment costs in other fields can also be reduced; this might largely eliminate any justification for higher admission standards for women training in a speciality.

Residual

The unexplained residual is defined as the differential earnings between men and women minus the differential earnings attributable to differences in the four productivity factors discussed. This residual is attributable to other factors which are identifiable on economic or other grounds but are not measurable in the absence of sufficient data. Thus, one part of the residual may be nondiscriminatory and another discriminatory. The nondiscriminatory part of the residual would include the earnings differential attributable to differences in job content and to exceptions to the equal pay for equal work principle. The discriminatory part of the residual constitutes the earnings differential attributable to prejudice and discrimination.

Table 4-2 shows a summary of this section for all and selected occupational groups in 1950, 1960, and 1970. Differences in earnings between men and women are adjusted by the four measurable factors, and the residual is also shown in column 8. Assuming that other costs are small, the differential earnings attributable to differences in job content and in exceptions to the Equal Pay Act of 1963, as amended, may constitute some portion of the residual; the remaining portion of the residual being the "unjustified" component of the income differential.

---

[n]Ideally, a method would be devised to identify better those among male as well as female applicants who are more likely to drop out.

Economic Implications of Court Decisions on Equal Pay for Equal Work

For a more precise determination of the "justified" and "unjustified" components of earnings differentials between men and women doing the same work, it is necessary to descend from the highly general census definition of occupation to more specific definitions of job content within a given occupation. This kind of detailed analysis of specific job content has been conducted largely in the courts. Although many of the judges making concrete decisions involving economic matters are not trained as economists, they may have a practical grasp of realities which makes their decisions of great value. It is often instructive for economists to descend from a general census category to a specific job definition, and to examine some of the concrete applications of the principle of equal pay for equal work made by the courts.

Definition of Equal Work

Equal work is work which involves "equality of the skill, effort, and responsibility required for performance and similarity of the working conditions under which they are performed."[19] In this definition, equal work is determined by job content rather than job title. Job content is determined by differences in skill, effort, responsibility, and working conditions.

Skill, which includes factors such as "experience, training, education and ability," is measured in terms of the "performance requirements of the job."[20] Possession of any other skills not required by the job cannot be taken into account in determining the quality of skill possessed for the job. Skill is defined as consisting of education, experience, and initiative and judgment in performing a specific job. When a male clerk spends his working time on typing and filing and his female counterpart on Xeroxing and computation, a question arises as to whether the male and female clerks possess equal skill or different skills. The answer depends on whether the operation of the calculator requires substantially more training than working on the copying machine. If the answer is in the affirmative, then a higher wage to the male clerk may be justified. But if the answer is not in the affirmative and training requirements are the same, then both male and female clerks possess comparable skill and should get equal pay.

Effort, which is another component in determining whether work performance is equal, is defined as "the degree or amount of the physical or mental exertion needed for the performance of the job."[21] For example, a male janitor cleans, waxes, and buffs floors while a female janitor cleans men's and women's rooms and dusts office furniture. The effort required for these two types of work does not appear to be substantially different and, therefore, would not justify a wage differential between the male and female janitors.

Responsibility, which is still another ingredient, is defined as "the degree of accountability required in the performance of the job with emphasis on the importance of the job obligation."[22] For example, a male payroll clerk checks time records and computes wages, while a female payroll clerk makes paychecks. The difference in responsibility between male and female payroll clerks is not considered substantial enough to justify a wage differential. But there is a considerable difference in the degree of the responsibility between male and female cashiers, if a female cashier is authorized to accept or reject payment for purchases by personal checks of customers while her male counterpart is not. Her added responsibility, which may affect the success of the business operation, may justify a wage differential.

Finally, similar working conditions may be judged "in the light of whether the difference in working conditions is the kind customarily taken into consideration in setting wage levels."[23] For example, when one electrician works inside a factory while another works in customers' homes, working conditions are dissimilar. But the difference in working conditions for the two is not large enough to justify a wage differential.

Exceptions to Equal Pay Standards

It is unlawful to apply different lines of advancement to male and female workers. It is also a violation of the Equal Pay Act to have a seniority system or line of progression which creates unreasonable obstacles to advancement by either sex into jobs of higher rank to which both sexes would be expected to get promoted. However, the Equal Pay Act provides three specific exceptions and one general exception under which a wage differential may be justified. These exceptions are: (1) a seniority system;[o] (2) a merit system;[p] and (3) a system measuring earnings by quality or quantity of productions.[q]

The second and third systems recognize productivity differences and really

---

[o]Under a seniority system senior employees get paid more than junior employees. The American Telephone and Telegraph Company and General Electric Company, and the U. S. Government, for example, employ such pay schedules.

[p]Merit pay differentials should reflect productivity differences, but often reflect other considerations. Merit rating tends to be determined by a superior who rates a subordinate's performance and recommends or disapproves a pay increase. The process tends to be nonobjective with the superior deciding for a variety of reasons whom he wants to favor with pay increases, and then figuring out what type of merit rating he must submit in order to justify the increase (Robert E. Sibson, *Wages and Salaries: A Handbook for Line Managers,* New York, American Management Association, 1967, pp. 92-6).

[q]This refers to an incentive or piece system in which workers get paid according to the qualtiy or quantity they produce. For example, if a male worker produces 100 needles while a female worker produces 110 needles, then the female would be paid more than her counterpart on economic grounds.

indicate unequal pay for unequal work on economic grounds, but the seniority system is a mixture of productivity and nonproductivity differences. The general exception provided by the Equal Pay Act refers to pay differentials based on any other factor than sex. Included are shift differentials, red circle rates, wage differentials for temporary and part time employment, and wage differentials under a training program.[r]

The success of the Equal Pay Act depends upon a proper interpretation of how equal jobs must be to warrant equal pay and to what extent additional duties make the work unequal and thereby justify a wage differential. Generally job evaluation takes two forms: (1) the traditional time and motion study in order to set a production standard; and (2) the method which weighs the relative worth of each job to the company in order to provide a ranking or grading of jobs. Since the latter method uses the components of skill, effort, responsibility, and working conditions, the Equal Pay Act requirements must be used to determine whether jobs performed by male and female workers are substantially equal in skill, effort, responsibility, and working conditions.

To measure the job content, relative weights must be assigned to each of the components of the job. The National Industrial Conference Board (NICB) made a survey of job evaluation in the 1940s to determine the relative weight of each of the four major components of a job. The Kress study of job evaluation is similar to the NICB survey in assigning a relative weight to each of the four components. The American Association of Industrial Management (AAIM) study is, however, more detailed and comprehensive than the previous studies by NICB and Kress.[s]

Court Decisions

The Department of Labor enforcement program of the Equal Pay Act of 1963

[r]Shift differentials: When only men happen to work on the night shift and women on the day shift, men may properly be paid a night shift differential.

"Red circle" rates: When a company wishes to transfer a long-service male (female) employee who can no longer perform his (her) regular job because of ill health to less demanding work which is now performed by employees who get paid less, the company properly pays the male (female) employee his (her) salary before the transfer. Such a salary is greater than that paid to the other employees doing the same work. But such a differential is considered proper.

Wage differentials for temporary and part time employees: When a temporary worker is employed during the Christmas season, he (she) may properly be paid less than permanent employees.

Wage differentials under a training program: An employee under a training program may be paid less though he (she) may perform the same work that already trained employees perform.

[s]Burton Dean and others report that the AAIM job evaluation is helpful in determining whether a job performed by male workers is different from that performed by female

was largely ineffective until the recent court decision of Shultz v. Wheaton Glass Company. The Wheaton case involved male and female workers who inspected and packed glass bottles on the assembly line. Male and female selector-packers performed the same work, but all males were paid 21½ cents (ten percent) more per hour than the females.[t]

The employer claimed that the "the male packers may be required to lift the heavy crates off the assembly line and place them on dollies or do various jobs requiring additional physical effort. The women selectors may work on the assembly line, selecting items, for example, and placing them in crates. This would be a significant difference which would justify a difference in pay."[24]

The court examined "additional tasks" performed by male selector-packers in some detail. These consisted of sixteen additional tasks such as lifting packages weighing more than 35 pounds, lifting cartons which are difficult to handle, operating hand trucks near the ovens, adjusting portable roller conveyers, and some other tasks pertaining to the selection and packing of glass bottles.

The court found no evidence that all male selector-packers performed any or all of these sixteen additional tasks. In fact, these extra tasks, when not performed by another category of employees known as "snap-up boys," were done by male selector-packers. The snap-up boys, who performed crating, moving bottles, and other unskilled miscellaneous tasks, were paid at the hourly rate of $2.16. The court also found that the male selector-packers spent an average of approximately 18 percent of their total working time on these extra tasks which were forbidden to women selector-packers.

Thus, the court concluded that availability of male selector-packers to perform the work of snap-up boys was an element of "flexibility." The claim of flexibility refers to transferability of work from snap-up boys to male selector-packers when snap-up boys are not available. In short, there was no finding of economic value in the element of flexibility sufficient to justify the 10 percent discrimination in pay rate between male and female selector-packers.

The significance of the Wheaton decision can be appreciated by comparison with the court decisions prior to the Wheaton case. An official count of equal pay cases tried by the Department of Labor prior to the Wheaton case showed that four cases were won and that eleven cases were lost.[25] The problem had been the failure to establish proper standards for determining whether men and women were performing equal work as defined by skill, effort, responsibility, and working conditions. As a result, the courts failed to interpret properly extra

workers. The AAIM job evaluation is based on four major factors with each major factor subdivided into several components. Each of the four factors has a relative weight. Skill is worth 50 percent, effort 15 percent, responsibility 20 percent, and working conditions 15 percent. See Burton Dean's article, "Job Evaluation Upholds Discrimination Suit," in *Industrial Engineering,* Vol. 3 (March, 1971), Table A.

[t]Female selector-packers were paid at an hourly rate of $2.14 which is ten percent less than the $2.35 rate. See 421 F. 2d 263 (1967).

work performed by men, permitting a wage differential between male and female workers based on "any factor other than sex."[u]

The Wheaton case has held that equal work means "substantially equal." Men spent 82 percent of their time performing equal work with women, the remainder of the time being spent on 16 additional manual tasks, and the court still found the job to be equal. It has become clear that the performance of certain additional duties by males such as lifting, stacking, and moving tasks will no longer justify higher pay when the nature of additional duties is more menial and involves less skill and responsibility than the regular tasks of the female workers.

A recent post-Wheaton decision indicates that the court has used more objective standards for determining whether men and women are performing equal work. In the American Can Company case, the appellate court found that the men on the third shift spent only two to seven percent of their time on the extra duties and concluded that male and female operators were performing equal work. Accordingly, the American Can Company decision of 1968 was reversed by the U.S. Court of Appeals in 1970.

The court has not yet faced the problem of affirming or reversing the Dennison case in 1967.[v] But the case is different from American Can or

---

[u]One example is provided: The American Can Company had a three-shift operation. Women worked on the first two shifts while men worked on the third shift at night. On the first two shifts all heavy work of bringing boxes to female machine operators was done by men. On the third shift male cup machine operators did this for themselves. Aside from this, there was no difference in skill, effort, responsibility, and working conditions between male and female machine operators.

Male machine operators were paid 20 cents an hour more than their female counterparts. The employer claimed that there was a significant difference in job content between cup machine operators on the first two shifts and cup machine operators on the third shift.

At first, the courts agreed with the company. However, the American Can Company decision of 1968 was reversed by the U.S. Court of Appeals in 1970 because "wage differential paying female operators 20 cents an hour less than male operators was not product of bona fide job classification system." For detail see *Wirtz v. American Can Co.*, 288 F. Supp. 20 (1968); and *Shutz v. American Can Co.*, 424 F. 2d 357 (1970).

---

[v]The Dennison Manufacturing Company plant in Framingham, Massachusetts had a three-shift operation. The third shift was all male while the first two shifts were all female. In addition to the regular operation of machines, each of the third shift male machine operators had to change over his machinery when necessary and also had to make repairs and adjustments when a machine was not operating properly. Men spent ten percent of their time on nonoperating duties. Further, each of the third shift male operators had to move his finished work to the shipping area, while female machine operators did not move their own materials to and from their machines.

The employer claimed that men on the third shift had to possess a significant degree of mechanical skill not required by women who could not or would not perform the mechanical duties.

The real issue is whether the difference in mechanical skill is insignificant or whether, as the employer claims, the difference is substantial enough to justify a wage differential between male and female operators.

The court concluded that the difference was substantial. The men on the third shift had to possess a significant degree of mechanical skill and ability. See 265 F. Supp. 787-790 (1967).

Wheaton Glass because the night operators in the Dennison Manufacturing Company were required to perform maintenance work without supervision, although a difference in pay rate between male and female operators based on extra duties performed by male operators is no longer approved by the courts.

"Justified" and "Unjustified" Income Discrimination

Our analysis in this chapter has shown, we believe, that differences in male-female productivity which are not in some sense a by-product of discrimination are relatively small. In the case of production and office work, the findings of the Bureau of Labor Statistics show almost insignificant differences in productivity. We are less certain about the situation in other occupations or fields of work, but upon close examination of the substantial difference found in scholarly productivity, we concluded that much of the productivity difference was due either directly or indirectly to some form of discrimination. Ultimately, when men and women have equal responsibility for the care of the household and of children, the productivity of women will be less adversely affected by career interruptions and other distractions. Whether most women will come to possess, as some now do, an aggressive and competitive spirit equal to that of the typical male can only be determined with further experience. Some differences in interests and capabilities may endure and some degree of career interruption cannot be avoided by women so long as they bear children, but the avoidable prejudice and biased reasons for productivity differences can be removed and the unavoidable differences minimized.

Our regression analysis appears to support these conclusions. If we correct for differences in hours worked, educational attainment, job seniority, and absenteeism, we can account for approximately one third of the difference between male and female earnings. The remaining two thirds, which are unexplained, may be the result of a variety of factors, such as extra costs of employing women, some of which are justified in economic terms and some of which are unjustified by any real differences in productivity or cost.

Unfortunately, census data are collected and cast in rather broad occupational categories which do not permit our coming to grips with the question of what proportion of the residual is due to bias, prejudice, and discrimination. Within each of the approximately 300 census occupational categories, latitude for legitimate pay differences due to productivity differences does exist—differences resulting from factors which are real and important but whose effects cannot be measured by regression equations or other means. This circumstance could lead to the conclusion that most of the unexplained two thirds of the difference between male and female earnings would be economically justified if we could properly determine the reasons for it.

Fortunately, we can examine the problem from another perspective, a perspective provided by court action, to determine whether the requirement of equal pay for equal work has or has not been met by an employer. These tests take the form specific legal actions brought by individuals or by the EEOC against employers believed to be guilty of discrimination. In most cases, the occupation under consideration is not broadly defined as in the census, but is very narrowly defined. Under scrutiny are men and women doing what in title, at least, is the same job. In fact, however, the work performed may be different. The critical issue, brought out by these cases, is whether the additional and different functions performed by men require more training, ability, or skill than the major job activity and, therefore, serve to justify higher rates of pay. Very specific instances of outright discrimination are often revealed in these cases, quite apart from the adverse effects upon earnings of women which stem from the entire discriminatory environment in which women have had to live and work. We can only conclude from an examination of these court decisions that a significant share of the unexplained differential is due to the discriminatory or sexist atmosphere which has characterized our society and culture up to the present time.

5 Factors Affecting Occupational Discrimination

This chapter attempts to analyze factors affecting under- or overrepresentation of women in certain occupations. Factors affecting demand and supply are examined, including discrimination in hiring and in the preparation of women for certain jobs or careers which are attributable to social and cultural conditioning.[a] Following a discussion of previous studies, we develop a measure of social and cultural discrimination as well as a measure of hiring discrimination in twenty fields. Departure from the fifty-fifty representation of men and women workers which distinguishes occupational discrimination is then separated into "justified" and "unjustified" components. Some recommendations which may reduce or eliminate occupational discrimination are made, and research areas which call for further investigation are indicated.

Hiring Requirements, Preferences, and Practices

While sex discrimination in employment is in violation of Title VII of the Civil Rights Act of 1964 with its various amendments, sex-segregated jobs still exist, products of employers' discriminatory hiring practices and the assignment of sex roles to men and women in our culture. This section deals with a brief survey of the literature on employers' hiring requirements, preferences and practices in selected occupations. Attention is focused on changes in such practices over time. Our survey is not intended to be comprehensive or exhaustive, but merely to indicate that flexibility exists in our culture which has permitted a gradual transformation of the social and cultural environment and implementation of social policies that were once considered to be impossible.

[a]Harriet Zeller in her article on "Discrimination Against Women, Occupational Segregation, and the Relative Wage," in *American Economic Review,* Vol. 62 (May, 1972), presents evidence that women are concentrated in low-paying occupations, but fails to indicate that occupational and income discrimination are not separable from social and cultural conditioning. This point, although not explicitly dealt with by Zeller, is discussed by Steven H. Sandell in "Discussion: What Economic Equality for Women Requires," in the same issue of the *American Economic Review.* Sandell believes that occupational and income equality will be achieved by developing in men and women a similarity of psychological attitudes toward life, work, tastes and preferences; a recognition of equal capabilities; and a resulting egalitarian style of marriage and an egalitarian society. In the same issue of the *Review,* Charlotte D. Phelps further supports egalitarian marriage and presents the "happiness function" based on an ability to give and receive love with proper self respect.

The Noland and Bakke Study

During 1945 and 1946 a survey was made by Professors Edward Noland and Edward Bakke of employers' hiring requirements, preferences, and practices in New Haven, Connecticut and Charlotte, North Carolina.[1] Employers were selected to represent all major industries in two areas. Five occupations were included in the survey: (1) production workers; (2) common laborers; (3) service and maintenance workers; (4) clerical workers; and (5) executive and administrative assistants.

Employers were asked to indicate their requirements and preferences with respect to the sex of the worker for various types of work. Men were required or favored in common labor, service and maintenance work, and administrative and executive work, while women were required or favored in clerical work. Production workers stood in the middle, depending upon the type of work performed by workers. If heavy work was involved, men were favored, but if light work was involved, women were favored.

The Noland and Bakke study indicated that sex was in fact of outstanding importance in the selection of an applicant. Individual capability was not given proper consideration by employers because of their traditional belief in the existence of men's and women's jobs.

The National Manpower Council Study

A report of seven conferences on hiring policies and practices affecting the employment of women, held by the National Manpower Council in 1955 and 1956,[2] presented findings which are consistent with the Noland and Bakke study but reveal that some changes had occurred in employers' attitudes toward women's capabilities in certain fields.

The reasons offered by the employers at these conferences for hiring or not hiring women may be divided into three broad categories or groups. The first category was the classification of jobs by the employers as "men's jobs" and "women's jobs" on the basis of tradition. The second category was based on the belief of employers that women workers possess certain characteristics or capabilities for certain kinds of work. The third set of reasons for not hiring women involved differences in labor costs between men and women workers. Employers pointed out that it costs more to employ women than men because more agreeable and comfortable working conditions as well as separate rest rooms must be provided for women. These three categories of objections to women employees were considered to be the key determinants of job opportunities for women in various occupations.

With respect to tradition, the employers unanimously pointed out that no factor was so influential in hiring practices as traditional job classification by sex. It was also evident that resistance to change in traditional practices has been substantial.

However, in the course of World War II, job opportunities for women expanded because of manpower shortages. Women replaced men in many blue-collar jobs such as operating drill presses, milling machines, lathes, punch and forming presses, and other machine tools. Experience showed that women did as well as men on light machine work. In the aircraft industry, for example, welding was considered a man's job before the war, but when women demonstrated that they were capable of doing good welding work, they were employed extensively in this occupation. But not all jobs permanently changed their male-female classification. When manpower shortages were alleviated after the war, many blue-collar jobs reverted to their former male classification, even though women had demonstrated their proficiency in the occupation.

The National Office Management Association Survey

A survey of hiring preferences and training programs was made by the National Office Management Association in 1960.[3] The survey included 1,900 business, industrial and service organizations in the United States and Canada. In the survey employers were asked to indicate their preferences with respect to the employment of equally qualified male and female workers. One third of the employers expressed no preferences. Employers who indicated female preferences were as numerous as those who preferred male workers. Some employers expressed special preferences for women 35 years of age and over because they felt that middle-aged women are dependable, require less training, and stay on the job longer than young women. The shortage of young women, though not a dominant factor, was also a contributing factor.

Nevertheless, most employers still prefer to promote a male over a female worker when both have equal job qualifications, although 44 percent of the employers indicated that they would not refuse to consider women for promotion. But equal chance of promotion still appears to be limited.

The Manpower Administration Study

In a recent survey of employers' hiring preferences and requirements in selected production and service occupations in major industries located in the New York and St. Louis areas,[4] more than eighty percent of employers indicated their preferences for men over women for the position of arc welder, orderly, press feeder, production machine operative, parts sales person, and shipping and receiving clerk, while most employers preferred women to men for bank teller and cashier-checker. No preferences were indicated in such occupations as hotel clerk and wire worker.

Although sex discrimination in each of these occupations was prohibited at the time the study was made, the influence of tradition was still pronounced and equal employment opportunity appeared limited.

The Schwartz Study

In an attempt to determine whether employers' hiring practices of women in management have changed, particularly since the Civil Rights Act of 1964, Eleanor Schwartz made a survey of women in managerial positions.[5] The survey covered 300 of the 750 firms listed in *Fortune* of June 15, 1968, representing the population of large business firms as well as 300 small firms, defined by the Small Business Administration, representing the population of small business firms.

More than half of employers (58 percent) recognized that women performed as well as men, and more than one quarter of employers (27 percent) said that women had no real problems in management. In small firms, however, nearly three-fourths of firms (73 percent) mentioned that women were better or as good as men, while nearly one-fifth of them (19 percent) were not satisfied with women.

Although most women evidently perform as well as men, women are still discriminated against in business according to Schwartz's findings. Nearly half of large firms (49 percent) and three-fourths of small firms (76 percent) admitted that women in management were discriminated against, while 70 percent of the women in management complained of discriminatory practices against women. Discrimination took a number of forms such as exclusion of women from executive training programs, lower pay, slower promotion, etc. Reasons cited for sex discrimination ranged from low aspiration and acceptance of a secondary role in management to reluctance on the part of women to file a discrimination charge for fear of damaging the employer-employee relationship or of losing a job.

The Schwartz study is highly instructive in providing the type of data needed for evaluating women in business. But more research on discriminatory hiring policies is required, before we can determine to what extent these are attributable to the absence or lack of experience of employers' in the employment of women, or to the attitude of women toward working in business management.

The Basil Study

Douglas C. Basil recently surveyed company and individual attitudes toward women in management in approximately 2,000 private companies and federal, state, and local agencies.[6] His findings show that women do not yet have equal opportunities for managerial and executive positions, although they perform as well as men. He then examined the attitudes of companies toward the promotion of women to managerial positions, and found that negative attitudes toward women as managers were deeply imbedded in our culture. Significant reasons given for these attitudes were pure prejudice, women's lack of emotional stability, and men's dislike of working for women. Basil also reported that discrimination against women was in large part attributable to women's lack of mobility, which is often necessary for a successful managerial or executive career. These findings are consistent with those of the Schwartz study.

Other Studies

Cynthia F. Epstein describes the professions as characterized by an "exclusive, club-like solidarity" which is a consequence of the sponsor-protegé relationship which prevails in much professional training.[7] Such a system has the consequence of excluding women, not because of inadequacies in their professional qualifications, but because they do not fit well into this type of system. As a result, the recruitment of women professionals is seriously limited. In her book, *Academic Women,* Jessie Bernard calls this type of exclusivity the "stag effect."[8] Often women are excluded from informal gatherings of discussions where pertinent scientific and technical information is exchanged among male scientists and engineers at cafeterias, snack bars, restaurants, or at social gatherings at private homes. The stag effect may, as a result, have an important bearing on the recruitment and advancement of women scientists and engineers.[9]

Experience of Western and Eastern Europe

Selected studies indicate that the social and cultural conditioning which tends to inhibit women has been and will be changed as more women are employed in the male-dominated professions. The experience of Western Europe in the employment of women, particularly career women, emphasizes that discrimination is both a short-run and long-run problem. As in the United States, the short-run issue is how to adapt employment practices to women's life cycle by providing maternity leave, child care facilities, part time employment and flexible hours, arrangement for relaunching highly qualified women whose careers have been temporarily interrupted, and the proper consideration of promotion associated with geographic relocation.[10] But the long-run issue that Britain and other Western European countries face is "not simply the removal of barriers to women's entry into a world of work which would otherwise remain unchanged, but the positive promotion of new attitudes and practices on the part of both men and women at work and in the family."[11] Only by such means can the climate within which women function be made to contribute to their improvement.

The Eastern European countries have moved a step further in this direction with the reduction or elimination of occupational discrimination through positive public policies. Women are actively recruited, trained, and given jobs in most areas of work. Indeed, in the Soviet Union in the 1920s positive discrimination was exercised to bring them into areas of work where they were underrepresented. Also a substantial quantity of child care facilities were provided in the public sector to reduce the burden of family responsibilities and free more women for work.[12]

Although the experience of Eastern Europe is not directly comparable to that of the United States, the United States is confronted with similar social and cultural problems. Like Western Europe we can gain insight from Eastern European experience, particularly in the areas of reshaping attitudes, developing effective nondiscriminatory policies, and providing facilities favorable to the employment of women in all fields of work.

The Effect of Social and Cultural Conditioning on the Employment of Women

Effect of Socialization on Males and Females

All societies define sex roles and form images of family and occupational life. Children are exposed to a set of expectations about themselves concerning what are acceptable occupational and family-social patterns. They absorb what occupations society considers to be of high value or low value. Thus, the culture of a society provides the framework within which its members are expected to behave and the norms to which they are expected to conform. This early conditioning plays a vital role in occupational choices. Some members who deviate from social expectations receive a mixed reception. Some will overcome the well-established values, norms, and images through determined struggles and continuous effort. Others will end up as failures because of their poor career planning and unavoidable and overwhelming difficulties.

This section attempts to explain the role of socialization in discrimination. By socialization is meant transmission of traditional values and norms about sex roles in various stages of human development. As young children develop, for example, boys are expected to be physically active and socially independent. They are often encouraged to be mentally alert and aggressive. On the other hand, girls generally receive more protection, more control, and more affection than boys. Girls are not always encouraged to be physically active and mentally alert.

As children grow older, sex-oriented training and expectations will be more explicitly introduced to boys and girls. Boys are encouraged to develop an interest in mathematics and science. When a boy shows remarkable progress in mathematics and physics, his father frequently suggests that he become a scientist. Girls, on the other hand, are encouraged to show an interest in the arts, music, and home economics. When a girl brings her excellent report card to her parents, she is likely to receive a different kind of treatment. She is appreciated by her parents, but is not considered as a would-be career woman to develop her individuality and self-fulfillment in her career. Implicit behind this kind of treatment is the ideology that woman's place is in the home.

This is only part of the story. A boy's long training in intellectual pursuit and independence and a girl's long training in passivity and dependence appear to influence the development of the intellectual functioning of each. Eleanor Maccoby has shown that there are few intellectual differences until about high school.[13] According to Maccoby, girls at this age are more likely to think of components as a functional whole; they will group together a doctor, a nurse, and a wheel chair because they all are associated with the care of sick people. Boys, on the other hand, are likely to associate one with another component on the basis of common characteristics. For example, people carrying suitcases are grouped together. This is what Jerome Kagan calls analytic grouping for boys and functional grouping for girls.[14] As a result, in high school girls begin to do worse in scientific subjects such as mathematics, chemistry, and physics because girls have developed an ability to handle information in a global manner, rather than in the analytic way needed for success in these fields.

In addition to sex differences in thinking between boys and girls affecting achievement and motivation in different fields, James Pierce has shown that high school girls have different criteria for achievement from boys.[15] Girls traditionally associate achievement with early marriage, whereas high school boys associate achievement with success in school. Further, M.S. Horner's study of undergraduates at the University of Michigan indicates that college women have what Horner calls a "motive to avoid success" because there is conflict with their concept of femininity.[16]

As these studies indicate, girls are confronted with a conflict between developing as would-be career women and playing the traditional role of women in the home, who are expected to be good-looking, charming, and sociable. Young girls are confronted with these two seemingly conflicting demands through their various stages of development.

A question then arises: Is it natural for girls to be conditioned differently from boys? If so, what would be the basic reason for this? To understand the problem, we shall review three types of argument, namely, the biological, psychological, and sociological.

The biological argument suggests that there exist inborn differences between men and women in developing potential ability which are caused by sex hormones. The problem with this argument is that it cannot explain why Russian women are different from American women in occupational distribution, particularly in professional occupations. A more satisfactory explanation must, therefore, be found elsewhere.

Another type of argument emphasizes psychological differences between men and women. This type of analysis is designed to measure differences between men and women in abilities and traits and to present measures of masculinity and femininity. Women are often assumed to possess characteristics such as emotional instability, lack of high intellectual ability, lack of extreme independence, lifetime devotion to family and to social work, substantial interest in grace, beauty, warmth, and peace. But the key issue boils down to what the factors determining psychological differences could be. Are these assumed differences primarily explained by biological factors such as sex hormones, chromosomes, and internal physiological organs, or by sociocultural factors attributable to sex-linked values in the family and in the economy and sex-oriented socialization processes in all stages of development? Or are they due to a combination of both? The authors, like Naomi Weisstein, subscribe to the theory that psychology constructs the female in the process of socialization.[17] Thus, sex-segregated occupations are primarily a historical product of social and cultural conditioning. In the modern world, physical factors which at one time may have played a part have largely been eliminated by mechanization. In socialistic countries such as Russia, Mainland China, and the Eastern European countries, women are encouraged to work outside the home in occupations usually typed as male in our society. In Russia, for example, propaganda has been effectively utilized to encourage women to participate in a number of occupations such as engineer, physician, machinist, plasterer, and tractor driver. Also the availability of child care facilities has enabled women to work in these and other occupations.[18]

In the United States, however, there is much less social pressure for women to work at all or in any specific occupations. Thus, women who attempt to demonstrate both feminine and masculine qualities, receive a mixed, if not hostile, reception. Nor is the American value system favorable to providing social and cultural support for women who would become professionals. Nevertheless, our system possesses flexible and pragmatic characteristics which favor change over time. It is in such a framework that decisions favoring careers for women can be made. There seems little doubt that the process of change in this regard is already in progress and that in the future young women will find many careers not only open to them but welcoming their participation.

Social and Cultural Discrimination and Discrimination in Hiring

Occupational discrimination is the result of two factors. The over- and underrepresentation of women in an occupation can be considered the sum of: (1) discrimination attributable to social and cultural conditioning or sex role socialization which prevents women from being adequately prepared for certain occupations; and (2) discrimination in hiring from among those qualified for a particular field of work. This section attempts to present and interpret both a measure of socially and culturally determined discrimination and a measure of discrimination in hiring.

In an effort to provide a measure of discrimination in twenty fields caused by social and cultural conditioning, the percentage of women who earned college or advanced degrees in each specialty during the 1940-68 period is measured. Should no social and cultural discrimination exist, the percentage of women trained in each specialty would be approximately 50 percent. Deviation from 50 percent in any field implies that social and cultural conditioning or sex role socialization has inhibited women's aspirations and prevented women from fully developing their capabilities in the area. When the proportion of women who are trained in engineering is, for example, three percent, the difference between 50 percent and 3 percent (47 percentage points) is attributable to social and cultural discrimination which discourages women from developing interests and abilities in the field of engineering. On the other hand, when the proportion of women among those who are trained in nursing is 95 percent, the difference between 50 percent and 95 percent (–45 percentage points) is also attributable to social and cultural discrimination, resulting from nursing being considered a woman's field rather than a man's. As a result, women are overrepresented in the field of nursing. Thus, our measure of social and cultural discrimination takes values between plus 50 percent and minus 50 percent. When the value of social and cultural discrimination is zero, no social and cultural discrimination exists. The more the value deviates from zero positively or negatively, the stronger is the social and cultural discrimination which distorts the equal representation of men and women in a field.

When no discrimination in hiring exists, the percentage of women who are employed should be approximately equal to the percentage of women who are trained. Of course, some women trained for a particular type of job or profession may not want to work in that field for a variety of reasons—family involvements, changed interests, etc. We make the assumption, however, that the difference between the percentage of women who are trained and the percentage of women who are employed is attributable to discrimination in hiring, when neither excess supply of nor excess demand for women exists. Discrimination in hiring is measured, therefore, by the difference between the percentage of those trained in a given field who are women, and the percentage of those who are employed in that field who are women, divided by the percentage of those trained who are women. As a result, discrimination in hiring may vary between zero—no discrimination in hiring—and one—maximum discrimination in hiring. Thus, the more the value deviates from zero, the stronger is discrimination in hiring.

As a starting point, consider that the proportion of women students who earned college or advanced degrees between 1940 and 1968, who were in the labor force in 1968, is much smaller than the proportion of men. The labor force participation rates for women college graduates were 58.4 percent and for men 90.4 percent.[19] Since the difference is 32 percentage points, discrimination in hiring would be above average in a field whose value in column 4 of Table 5-1 is greater than 32, and less than average in a field whose value is less than 32.

Second, the occupations which women actually enter may not be directly related to those fields in which they earned their degrees. This situation may occur either when women seek employment but cannot find jobs directly related to their respective fields, or when they shift to another occupation not directly related to the fields in which they were trained. In either case the potential supply of women may change in response to the labor market situation. The critical issue is whether there is a significant difference between the potential supply of women and the actual supply of women in each field. If the difference is considerable, a measure of discrimination in hiring does not present properly the degree of occupational discrimination. If, on the other hand, the difference between potential supply and actual supply of women is relatively small in each field, our measure of discrimination in hiring would represent properly the degree of discrimination. In the absence of data on this point, it is impossible to determine whether the difference between the potential and actual supply varies considerably with fields, but we assume that the difference is small.

Third, selection of the proper universe for the determination of the percentage of women who are trained as opposed to those who are employed is critical to provide a meaningful measure of what, for convenience, we call social and cultural discrimination. This type of problem is not a serious one for us because data compiled by the Office of Higher Education, Department of Health, Education and Welfare are very close in coverage to those data compiled by the Bureau of Labor Statistics.

Fourth, estimates of the percentage of male and female college graduates who are employed in each field are important to provide a measure of discrimination in hiring. Data from the Bureau of the Census and the Bureau of the Labor Statistics are employed to represent the proper universe of the population.

The precise extent to which women's exclusion from certain fields at specialized training is the result of sex discrimination in admissions as compared to self-imposed exclusion as a result of sex role socialization is difficult to determine. Discrimination in medical schools has been notorious; in other areas it has been less.[20] The overriding factor deterring women from entering most fields is the social and cultural conditioning which inhibits their aspirations. Column 3 of Table 5-1 shows that the impact of social and cultural discrimination is substantial in the male-dominated fields such as dentistry, medicine, law, and engineering. Among these twenty fields, social and cultural discrimination is strongest in dentistry (48), followed by engineering (47), law

(46), physics (45), geology (44), medicine (43), computer science (40), economics (40), pharmacy (35), chemistry (32), political science (30), biological

Table 5-1
Social and Cultural Discrimination and Discrimination in Hiring in Selected Fields, 1968

Field	*Percentage of Women among Trained 1940-68*[a] *(1)*	*Percentage of Women among Employed 1968* *(2)*	*Social & Cultural Discrimination*[b] *(3)*	*Discrimination in hiring*[c] *(4)*
Natural Science				
Mathematics	30	11	20	62
Computer Science	10	10	40	0
Physics	5	4	45	20
Chemistry	18	7	32	61
Geology	6	3	44	50
Biological Sciences	27	13	23	52
Health				
Dentistry	2	2	48	0
Medicine	7	7	43	0
Nutrition	98	90	−48	8
Nursing	96	95	−46	1
Pharmacy	15	8	35	46
Engineering	3	1	47	66
Social Science				
Economics	10	6	40	40
History	45	10	5	77
Political Science	20	10	30	50
Sociology	56	12	− 6	78
Psychology	43	24	7	44
Other Science				
Library Science	95	85	−45	10
Humanities				
Social Work	59	50	− 9	15
Law	4	4	46	0

[a] Includes bachelor's, master's, doctor's, and professional degrees.

[b] Social and cultural discrimination equals 50 minus column 1. It is zero if men and women are equal in number. The maximum discrimination against women (men) is plus (minus) 50, indicating that those who were trained are all men (women).

[c] Hiring discrimination is (col. 1 – col. 2)/col. 1 x 100. It is zero if all women who were trained are hired. The maximum discrimination is 100 if no women who were trained are hired.

Sources: Bureau of the Census, *Statistical Abstracts of the United States* in various years; Department of Health, Education and Welfare, Chapter on *Statistics of Higher Education;* Bureau of Labor Statistics, *College Educated Workers, 1968-1980* (Bulletin 1678, 1970).

sciences (23), and mathematics (20). Mild social and cultural discrimination exists in social work (–9), psychology (7), and sociology (–6). In contrast nutrition (–48), nursing (–46), and library science (–45) are three fields in which women are concentrated. Overrepresentation of women in each of these fields represents discrimination in reverse.

Column 4 shows that discrimination in hiring is strongest in sociology (78), followed by history (77), engineering (66), mathematics (62), chemistry (61), biological sciences (52), pharmacy (46), psychology (44), and economics (40). Discrimination in hiring is mild in physics (20), social work (15), library science (10), and nutrition (8). Almost no discrimination in hiring exists in nursing (1). No discrimination in hiring exists in computer science (0), dentistry (0), medicine (0), and law (0).

To interpret discrimination in hiring properly, it is necessary to separate it into "justified" and "unjustified" components. As an example, consider that the percentage of women of working age who are college graduates is 50 percent and that the percentage of these women who chose not to work is one half (25 percent of those of working age). Further, the proportion of women graduates who are employed is two-fifths (20 percent of the working age group). Finally, we assume that half of these women college graduates do not seek full time or part time employment. Under these conditions the difference between the percentage of women of working age who are college graduates and seek employment (25 percent) and the percentage of women who are college graduates and are employed (20 percent) is 5 percent. This 5 percent is an "unjustified" component of discrimination in hiring, attributable to employers' discriminatory hiring practices.

"Justified" and Unjustified" Occupational Discrimination

In the absence of data on the labor force participation rate of women college graduates by field, it is impossible to separate discrimination reflected in low participation rates into "justified" and "unjustified" components in each field. It is instructive, however, to indicate in which field the "unjustified" component of discrimination in hiring is likely to be greater, by comparing participation rates in individual fields with the average, based on the labor force participation rate of women college graduates.

As mentioned earlier, the difference in the labor force participation rate between men and women college graduates in 1968 was 32 percentage points (90.4-58.4 percent). As will be discussed in Chapter 6, an estimate of temporary withdrawal of women from the labor force during the childbearing and child-rearing period amounts to 3 to 4 percent of the labor force participation rate of women.[b] This figure is considered to be a "justified" component of

---

[b]For a full discussion see pages 92-94.

discrimination in hiring on physiological grounds. Thus, the difference between 32 percent and 3 to 4 percent, or 28 to 29 percent, is due to "unjustified" discrimination in hiring, if we assume that ultimately women will have a desire to work equal to that of men. But at a given stage of historical development such as the present, the 28 to 29 percentage point figure may be justified on the grounds that women do not choose to participate in the labor force more than they do. If we assume this to be the case today, the "unjustified" component of discrimination in hiring attributable to employers' discriminatory hiring practices can be obtained by subtracting 3 to 4 percent as a "justified" component on physiological grounds, and 28 to 29 percent or a total of 32 percent, as a temporarily "justified" desire for nonparticipation. Making this adjustment to column 4 of Table 5-1, we find that among twenty fields "unjustified" discrimination in hiring is greatest in sociology (46), followed by history (45), engineering (34), mathematics (30), chemistry (29), biological sciences (19), geology (18), political science (18), pharmacy (14), psychology (12), and economics (8). In the remaining fields, "unjustified" discrimination in hiring shows negative values, indicating that no "unjustified" discrimination exists. These fields are physics (−12), social work (−17), library science (−22), nutrition (−24), nursing (−31), computer science (−32), dentistry (−32), medicine (−32), and law (−32).

Any "unjustified" component of occupational discrimination can be eliminated by a number of correctional measures. For example, social and cultural discrimination, which adversely affects the supply of women, can be reduced or eliminated by a long-term program of education. Such a program would call for basic changes in well entrenched attitudes and patterns of behavior as well as more concrete measures. For example, although women may be as qualified as men, some of them have psychologically accepted a secondary role in their professions because they lack confidence or because their primary concern is with their family. Only with the removal of psychological constraints, as well as family burdens, can one important factor that leads to discrimination be removed. Women's rights organizations, especially on campuses, can provide critical moral support in this regard.[21] A redefinition of the role of married women in the family is also required. The true egalitarian marriage allows both husband and wife to pursue careers outside the home. Then both will provide for the care of children, a role which has traditionally fallen on the female partner. The egalitarian marriage also affects the distributive burden of household work and the decision-making process between husband and wife.[c] The dual worker family

[c]In France the hypothesis that the dual-worker family is more egalitarian than the one worker family was separated into four subhypotheses and each subhypothesis was tested and was statistically significant. The four subhypotheses were: (1) the decision-making process is more egalitarian in the dual-worker family than in the one worker family; (2) the decision-making process is less specialized in the dual-worker family than in the one worker family; (3) the division of household work between husband and wife is more egalitarian in the dual-worker family than in the one worker family; and (4) the household tasks are less specialized in the dual-worker family than in the one worker family. For detail see Andree

tends to be more egalitarian than the one worker family in handling joint decisions between husband and wife.[d] Perhaps the most important and difficult problem in making a joint decision between husband and wife is an occupational choice. Suppose both wife and husband earned Ph.D. degrees in their respective fields and the husband is offered a job as a psychiatrist in Los Angeles, while the wife is teaching sociology in Boston. Without questioning the basic happiness of such a dual career marriage, either husband or wife must make a sacrifice if they want to live together. Either the husband or wife must seek his or her second best employment in the Los Angeles or Boston area Thus, for some appreciable change in the nature of the family as an institution is required for the pursuit of dual careers.

The provision of additional social services and changed work regimes is also important in reducing the burden on the dual worker family.[22] These should include the broader provisions of child care facilities, flexible working hours, more extensive use of shift and part time work, and flexible business hours to provide services at the convenience of consumers.

These provisions will encourage the move toward the egalitarian dual career family and a society in which training, education, employment, pay, fringe benefits, promotion, layoff, termination, and other conditions of employment for women in all private and public institutions or organizations at all levels must be substantially comparable, if not entirely identical, to those of their male counterparts. To accomplish these broad objectives, we shall face some critical social and economic issues and problems each of which requires proper solution. Above all, nothing would be more important and effective in making a social and cultural climate favorable to women workers than social legitimation of the dual worker family through the various means of mass communication.[23] The solution will call for changes in attitudes and behavior which are not easy to achieve, but a country so successful at selling soap, cigarettes, or presidents should be able to affect the public thinking positively on many of these issues.

Michel, "Interaction and Goal Attainment in Parisian Working Wives' Families," in *Family Issues of Employed Women in Europe and America*, K. Ishwaran, ed., Leiden, the Netherlands, Brill, 1971, pp. 43-65.

In Germany Annette Lamouse, "Family Roles of Women: A German Example," in *Journal of Marriage and the Family,* Vol. 31, February, 1969, pp. 145-52, confirms the hypothesis similar to French experience.

In Poland, however, the above hypothesis is not statistically significant, though the dual-worker family is slightly more egalitarian than the one worker family. Jerry Piotrowski attributes the primary reason to the persistence of cultural lag between behavior determined by social and cultural relations on one hand and that determined by traditionally male dominated family relations. For detail see "The Employment of Married Women and the Changing Sex Roles in Poland," *Family Issue of Employed Women in Europe and America, op. cit.,* pp. 77-90.

---

[d]In their recent book, Rhona and Robert Rapopport emphasize the necessity of social legitimization of the dual worker family rather than the traditional one worker family in accelerating a social change favorable to women. For detail see their *Dual Career Families,* London, Penguin Books, 1971.

Effective action on more specific short-range goals would also be desirable. Vigorous efforts are required by the Presidential Commission on the Status of Women, the Equal Employment Opportunity Commission, and women's organizations such as the American Association of University Women, National Organization for Women, National Federation of Business and Professional Women's Clubs, Women's Equity Action League, and other similar organizations to achieve:

1. Equal employment opportunity.
2. Equal pay for equal work.
3. Equal consideration for promotion and layoff.
4. Special protection of women through provisions for maternity leave.
5. Job guarantees after maternity leave.
6. Strict enforcement of the EEOC guidelines in relation to the state protective laws.
7. Equal treatment of women in job training.
8. Enforcement of federal contract compliance.
9. Tax reforms permitting the deduction of child care expenses by working mothers.
10. Equal treatment of women in pension and retirement benefits.
11. Increased appointive positions in government.
12. Affirmative action programs in institutions of higher education and in the business and professional community, to rectify disproportionate male-female distribution in employment.

Further research in the area of occupational discrimination is also needed. Some of the areas which hold promise for further investigation include development of an adjusted index of discrimination in hiring on the proportion of professionals who are women, either holding jobs or seeking employment in a given field, rather than on the proportion of women degree holders in the field; since possession of a degree is not necessarily indicateve of a continuing desire to work in the field.

Fortunately, the National Science Foundation study, *American Science Manpower 1970*, provides the numbers of men and women registered in each scientific and professional field. Those who are registered, as opposed to those with degrees, can be presumed to consider themselves active members of the profession and either employed or seeking employment in their special field of work. If we compare the proportion of those registered in a field who are women with the proportion of women among those empoloyed, we obtain a more accurate index of discrimination in hiring. For example, the proportion of registered biologists who are women was 12.9 percent compared with 12.2 percent of the work force in this field. If we compare the index of discrimination in hiring based on the proportion of registered biologists who are women, as opposed to those trained, we obtain 5.5. The difference between our index of 52 (column 4 of Table 5-1) and 5.5 is then attributable primarily to voluntary dropouts form the field due to factors such as marriage, family responsibilities, changes in career interests, etc.; but also in many cases women may have withdrawn from a field because they suffered from so much disappointment as a result of discrimination in various forms that they became unwilling to continue.[e]

To accomplish this objective it is necessary to develop data on employment by sex, detailed occupation, level of academic degree, work experience, and type of employer. The National Science Foundation publications *American Science Manpower 1970* and *Unemployment Rates and Employment Characteristics for Scientists and Engineers 1971* provide some of the needed data. Other data on employment by occupation and sex from the Bureau of Labor Statistics, Bureau of the Census, the Manpower Administration, and the Equal Employment Opportunity Commission are still inadequate, in the absence of the qualitative data such as those found to some extent in the NSF publications.

In institutions of higher education in particular, a number of troubling problems in evaluating affirmative action plans exist.[24] In drawing up these plans one approach has been to develop data to enable the Office of Civil Rights (OCR) to determine whether women show under-, over, or fair representation in each specialty, provided that women are available with equivalent education, professional experience, and other relevant characteristics. The proportion of persons registered by field or profession who are women in the NSF study would be helpful in this regard. The index of adjusted discrimination in hiring indicated here would provide a specific goal or target to be used in evaluating affirmative action plans in terms of nondiscrimination in hiring, as opposed to occupational discrimination in the larger sense of the discouragement of women from obtaining the kind of training needed to enter a field. However, a blanket application of targets based on the NSF data may not be desirable. The OCR should not ignore the qualitative dimensions of the problem. The NSF data do not show the academic ranks of those registered or their qualifications for various scientific or professional responsibilities.

We have observed that one of the serious obstacles to married women with qualifications equivalent to men in executive and administrative positions not receiving equal treatment is the problem of their reduced mobility, either

[e]Similar computation for fifteen fields based on the percentage of women registered in a field minus the percentage of women employed in that field divided by the percentage of women registered will be listed in the descending order: physics (16.2); mathematics (11.4); earth sciences (11.4); computer science (10.8); economics (10.0); linguistics (9.7); statistics (7.8); political science (7.2); atmospheric sciences (6.6); sociology (6.6); chemistry (5.6); biology (5.5); psychology (5.4); anthropology (4.6); and agricultural sciences (.01). For detail see *American Science Manpower 1970*, Tables A-1, A-8, and A-62.

temporarily or permanently, should the need for a move to another area arise. It is necessary to examine this type of occupational discrimination to determine whether part of such discrimination can be justified or not, either in the short or the long run.

6

Factors Affecting Participation Discrimination

The remarkable increase in the number of women workers over the past five decades shows the effects of changing demographic, economic, social, and legal conditions on the participation of women in the labor force. This chapter attempts to investigate the effect of the following on the participation of women in the labor force: (1) demographic factors; (2) the demand for and supply of women in the labor force; (3) the burden of household work; (4) husbands' attitudes toward wives working outside the home; (5) federal laws and regulations concerning sex discrimination; and (6) physiological differences between men and women which distinguish "justified" and "unjustified" components of nonparticipation. Research topics on the participation of women in the labor force, which are considered to be significant and worthy of investigation, are briefly indicated.

Demographic Factors

Past studies demonstrate that demographic factors explain little of the rise in the labor force participation of women. A study by John Durand of the 1920-40 period shows that changes in demographic factors such as the distribution of the female population by age, region, color-nativity, marital status, and the presence or absence of one or more children made an insignificant contribution to the rise in the labor force participation of women.[1] Seymour Wolfbein and A.I. Jaffe also examined changes in demographic factors, such as the distribution of the female population by age and marital status between 1890 and 1930, and concluded that the influence of these factors was small compared with that of other social and economic factors.[2] In a 1960 study, Stanley Lebergott concluded that social and economic factors, rather than demographic factors, explain the increase in female employment.[3]

A more recent study by Valerie Oppenheimer shows the effect of changing population composition on the labor force participation of white females in the period between 1920 and 1960.[4] In the 1920-40 period the net positive effect of changes in age composition, urban-rural residency, and marital status on the participation rate of white women in the labor force accounted for only one-tenth of one percent, compared with 3.9 percent for other factors. For the 1950-60 period, changes in age composition and marital status again contributed to a decrease in the participation rate of women in the labor force, while urban residency accounted for a small rise in the participation of women in the labor force. The net effect of these demographic variables on the participation rate was minus 1.3 percent, whereas other factors accounted for plus 6.9 percent during this period. The relatively small net effect of demographic factors on the rise in the labor force participation of women shown in the earlier studies, is confirmed by this very recent study by Oppenheimer. Nevertheless, it is instructive to look into the effect of each demographic variable.

Age Composition and Age-Marital Status

We will begin by separating the effect of changes in age composition and age-marital status on the participation of women in the labor force from the effect of changes in other factors on the participation rate. Our method is based on the assumption that the female labor force participation rates by 10-year age groups and by age-marital status remain unchanged between the base year and the year to be compared. The expected labor force participation rates in 1940 can be calculated by multiplying the 1940 distribution of the female population by age-marital status by the corresponding 1920 participation rates. This provides the expected participation rate for women in 1940 when only the distribution of women by age-marital status has changed, but no change has occurred in the actual participation rate due to a change in the desire or need for women to work in any of the age-marital status groups. The difference between the expected participation rate in 1940 and the actual participation rate can be attributed, therefore, to factors other than age-marital composition.

The effect of age-marital composition on the labor force participation rates of women for the 1920-40 period shows that the change in the age-marital composition of the female population would have caused a decline in the labor force participation rate by 2.2 percent, while factors other than age-marital composition would have accounted for a 4.9 percent increase, resulting in a net increase of 2.7 percent.[a] An increase in the participation rate of married women in the labor force from 9.0 percent to 13.8 percent is attributable to age composition (–.5 percent) and other factors (5.3 percent). A decrease in the participation rate of other women in the labor force from 46.4 percent to 43.5 percent is attributable to age composition (–7.4 percent) and other factors (4.5 percent).

What, then, would be the reason for the increase in the labor force participation rate of women during the 1920-40 period? During this period the participation of women in the labor force showed an increase of 2.7 percent from 23.7 to 26.4 percent. This change was due to significant increases in the labor force participation rates of younger women. In 1920 the labor force

---

[a]4.9 minus 2.2 = 2.7 for all women, 1920-40 (Table 6-1).

participation rate of girls in the 14-19 age group was 32.7 percent. The participation rate of women in the 20-24 age group, when most women had completed their schooling and were either unmarried or childless if married, increased to 38.1 percent. The rate then dropped to 18 percent for women in the 25-44 age group and steadily decreased to only 19 percent at 55 years old and over. As shown in Figure 6-1, the 1920 female labor force participation may be characterized as the inverted V shape with a peak in the 20-24 age group.

In 1940 only 18.9 percent of girls in the 14-19 age group were in the labor force, indicating that more girls at that age were in school than in 1920. The participation rate of women in the 20-24 age group also reached a peak of 45.6 percent, a significant increase by 7.5 percentage points over the twenty year period. The participation rate then fell steadily with each age group, dropping to only 6.1 percent at 65 years of age and older. The 1940 participation pattern can also be described as the inverted V shape with a peak in the 20-24 age group.

The significant difference between the participation pattern in 1920 and 1940 is, however, that the proportion of women in the labor force was larger in 1940 than in 1920 except the 14-19 age group. That is, the entire inverted V pattern is moved upward except for the 14-19 age group. This upward shift itself accounts for the negative effect of changing age and age-marital status on the labor force participation rates of women, because the 1920 distribution of the female working age group is assumed to be unchanged in 1940.

For the period between 1940 and 1960 the proportion of children under 15 years of age in the population increased from 25 to 30 percent, and the proportion of older people over 64 years of age increased from 7 to 10 percent. As a result, the proportion of the female working age group showed a decline from 68 to 60 percent. But the observed labor force participation rate of women in the 14-64 age group increased by a substantial 10.6 percentage points from 27.7 to 38.3 percent. The labor force participation rate of single women declined slightly from 46.4 to 44.3 percent. This decline was more than offset by the increase in the labor force participation rates of married women and women of other marital status. In particular, there was a significant increase in the percentage of married women in the labor force from 14.4 to 32.6 percent. The labor force participation of women of other marital status also increased from 47.3 to 58.3 percent.

Between 1940 and 1960 the pattern of participation changed significantly in shape. In 1940 the pattern was an inverted V shape. In 1960 the pattern achieved the classic M shape. The M shape indicates that there are two peaks in the participation rates, one at age 20 to 24, and the other at age 45 to 49, with the participation rate falling after age 25 during the childbearing years, and then increasing at age 30 to 34 and decreasing again after age 50 (Figure 6-1).

An examination of participation patterns by marital status reveals that participation rates of married women with husband present changed significantly between 1940 and 1960. In 1940 the participation pattern is described as the

Table 6-1
The Effect of Changing Age Composition and Marital Status on the Labor Force Participation Rates of Women, 1920-60 (in percent)

Labor Force Participation Rate	*1920-1940*		
	Total[a]	*Married*[b]	*Others*[c]
1. 1920 (observed)	23.7	9.0	46.4
2. 1940 (observed)	26.4	13.8	43.5
3. 1940 (expected)	21.5	8.5	39.0
4. Due to Changes in:			
Age Composition (line 3 – line 1)	– 2.2	– .5	– 7.4
Other Factors (line 2 – line 3)	4.9	5.3	4.5

	1940-1960			
	Total[d]	*Married*[b]	*Single*[e]	*Others*[f]
1. 1940 (observed)	27.7	14.4	46.4	47.3
2. 1960 (observed)	38.3	32.6	44.3	58.3
3. 1960 (expected)	26.5	14.0	38.5	45.8
4. Due to Changes in:				
Age Composition (line 3 – line 1)	– 1.2	– .4	– 7.9	1.5
Other Factors (line 2 – line 3)	10.6	18.6	5.8	12.5

[a]Includes participation rate of all women. Participation rates are calculated by ten year age cohorts, 15 and over.

[b]Includes married women with husband present.

[c]Includes single women never married, women who are divorced, separated, widowed, and women whose husbands are not present.

[d]Includes participation rate of all women. Participation rates are calculated by ten year age cohorts, 14 to 64.

[e]Women who are never married.

[f]Includes women who are divorced, separated, widowed and women whose husbands are not present.

Source: Bureau of the Census, *1920 Census of Population,* Vol. 4, Chapter 6, Tables 5 and 6; *1940 Census of Population,* Vol. 2, Part 1, U.S. Summary, Table 8; *1960 Census of Population,* Vol. 2, Part 6, Table 6.

inverted V shape with one peak at age 25 to 29 (Figure 6-2). In 1960, however, the participation pattern is characterized as M shape with two peaks, one reaching 26 percent at age 20 to 24 and the other 39.3 percent at age 45 to 54. As for single women the participation pattern did not show much change between 1940 and 1960, except that more single women stayed on the job after age 30 in 1960 than in 1940 (Figure 6-3). Women of other marital status (divorced, separated, widowed, and married with husband absent) also showed the inverted V shape. The participation rate reached a peak of 66.6 percent at age 30 to 34 in 1940, compared with a peak of 69.1 percent at age 45 to 54 in 1960. That is, the inverted V shape shifted upward and to the right (Figure 6-4). More women of other marital status at age 35 and over stayed on the job in 1960 than in 1940, while more women of other marital status at age 20 to 34 participated in the labor force in 1940 than in 1960.

In 1970 the M shape pattern of participation was moved further upward. The first peak of 56.9 percent was at age 20 to 24, and the second peak of 54.0 percent was at age 45 to 54. An examination of the female labor force participation by marital status also shows that the participation of married women of all ages increased significantly from 30.6 percent in 1960 to 40.8 percent in 1970 (Figure 6-2). The participation of single women also increased from 42.9 percent to 53.0 percent. Significant increases in the participation rates at age 14 to 19 and 25 to 29 were more than offset by decreases in the participation rates at age 20 to 24 and 30 and over. The participation of women of other marital status showed a slight increase from 38.7 in 1960 to 39.1 percent in 1970.

Implicit in these changes in the pattern of participation of women in the labor force from the inverted V shape to the M shape are changes in the life cycle of married women. In the late nineteenth century girls went to school until they were 14 or 15, worked for seven to eight years until they were married at age 22, and then withdrew from the labor force permanently. In comparison with the life cycle pattern of married women in the late nineteenth century, in 1960 young women started their first jobs at age 17 or 18 when they completed high school, worked until they were married at age 20 or 21 and had children a few years later, and returned to work after age 40 when their children were grown up. This 1960 life cycle pattern of married women was similar to that of married women in 1970, except more married women continue to work or return to the labor force at an earlier age.[5]

Results shown in Table 6-1 are consistent with those of Durand, Wolfbein and Jaffe, Lebergott, and Oppenheimer. In particular, changes in the participation pattern of women during the period between 1920 and 1970 were significant. More married women after age 35 were in the labor force in 1970 than any other previous census year.

Supply of and Demand for Women[b]

This section analyzes factors affecting the supply of married women, the supply

---

[b] A detailed discussion of the supply of married women, the supply of single women, and the demand for women is found in Appendix C.

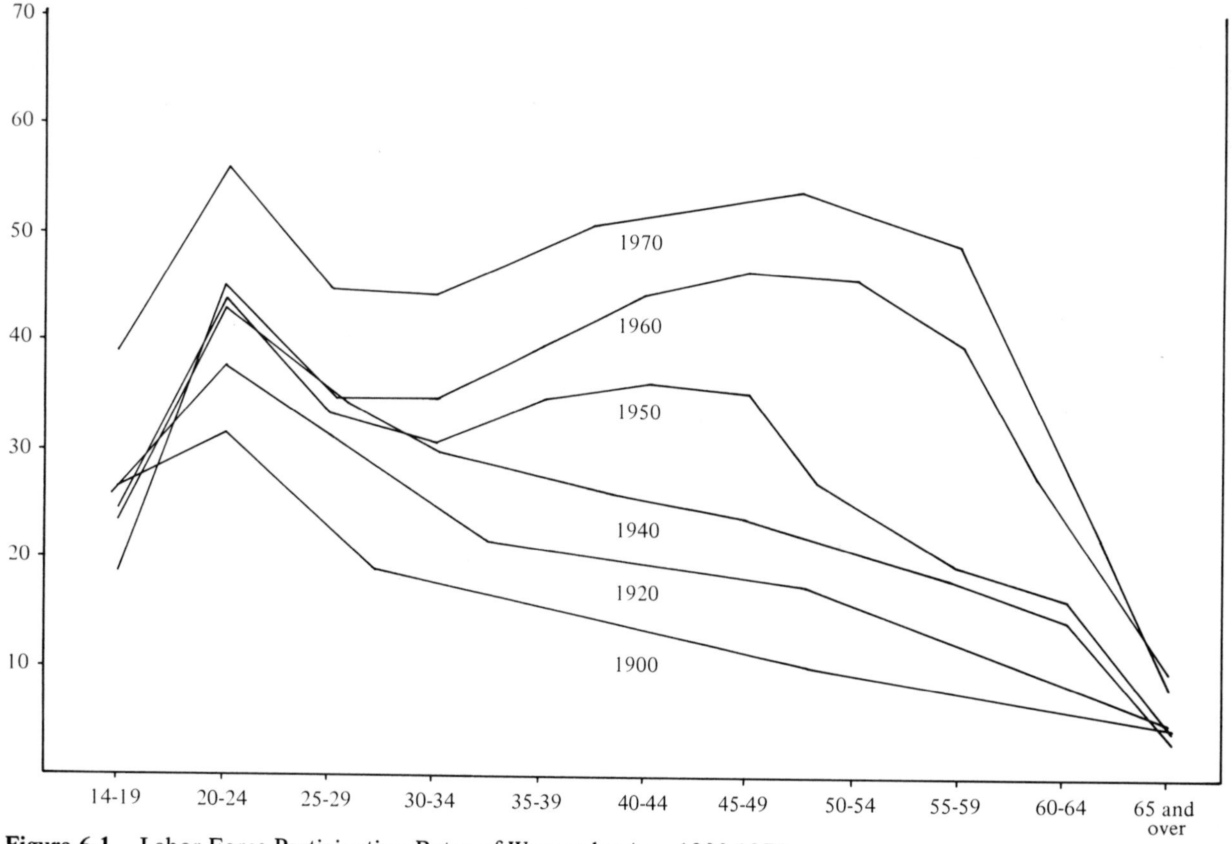

Figure 6-1. Labor Force Participation Rates of Women by Age, 1900-1970.

Source: See Appendix B, Table B-1.

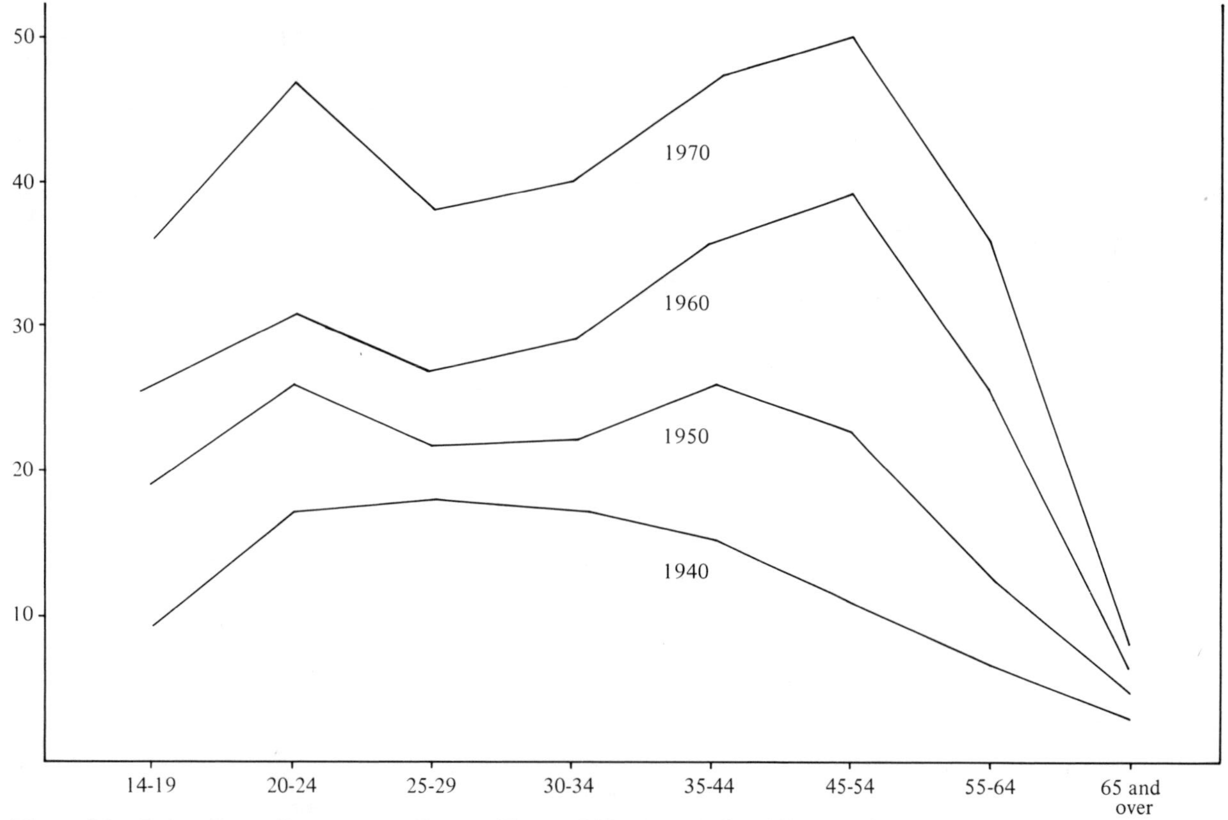

Figure 6-2. Labor Force Participation Rates of Married Women, Husband Present, by Age, 1940-70.

Source: See Appendix B, Table B-2.

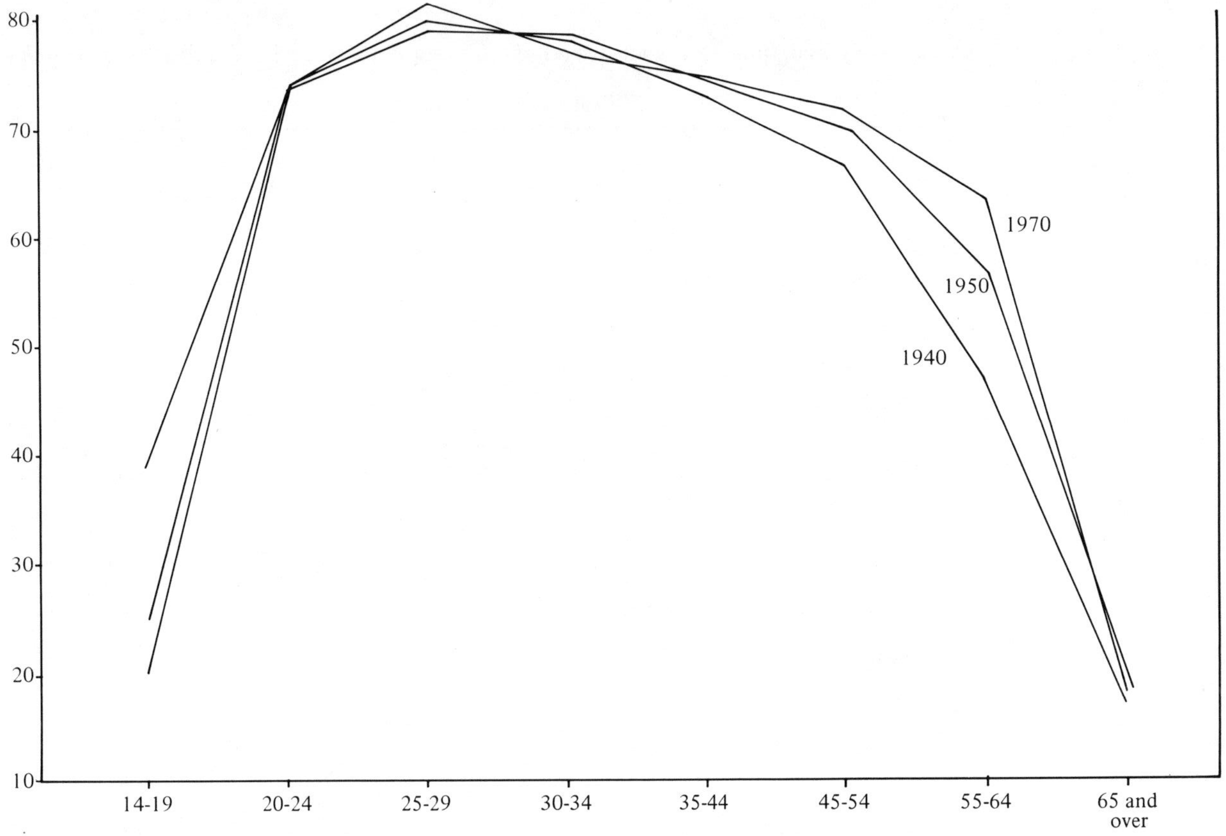

Figure 6-3. Labor Force Participation Rates of Single Women by Age, 1940-70.

Source: See Appendix B, Table B-2.

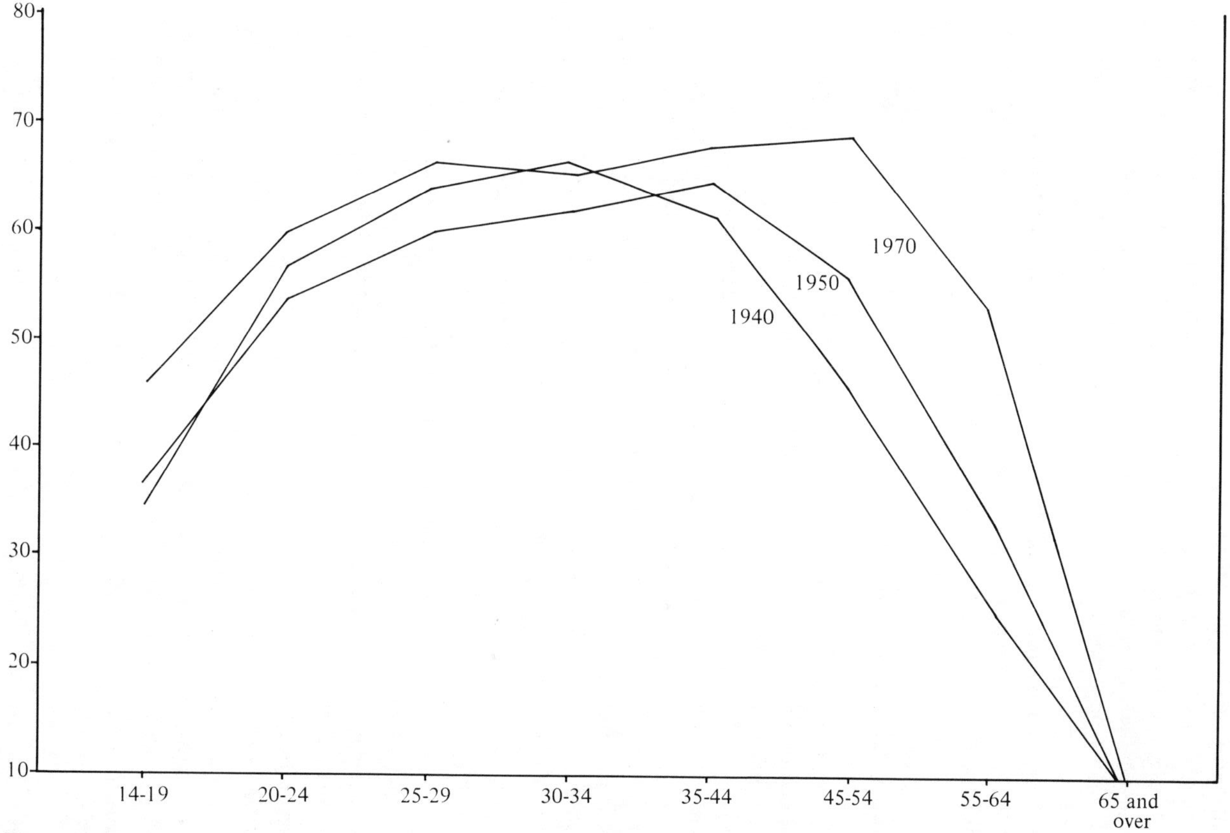

Figure 6-4. Labor Force Participation Rates of All Other-Ever-Married Women by Age, 1940-70.

Source: See Appendix B, Table B-2.

of single women, and the demand for women. Regression technique (the ordinary least sqaures method) was employed to derive estimates of regression coefficients in each equation.

Regarding the supply of married women, our purpose is to determine whether the effect of wives' income on their supply is greater than that of husbands' income on the supply of wives, and to show that educational attainment and employment opportunity are the two most important factors explaining the increase in the participation of married women in the labor force. This hypothesis is true for the supply of single women as well. The demand for women is then analyzed to determine that the educational and employment hypothesis is supported on the demand side.

Supply of Married Women

We have included in our regression a set of standard variables. The labor force participation rate of married women with husband present was made a function of the husband's income, the wife's income, nonlabor income, educational attainment, the male unemployment rate, and child care cost. Our results were found to be consistent with those by Mincer, Cain, Bowen and Finegan, and Cipriani. However, there is some serious question as to whether this approach is entirely valid. Therefore, our results shown in Appendix C must be viewed with some reservations.

On the basis of these results, however, we have obtained some interesting, although not entirely surprising, conclusions:

1. The lower a husband's income, the higher the labor force participation rate of his wife.
2. The lower the nonlabor income of a family, the higher the labor force participation rate of a married woman.
3. The higher the income a working wife receives, the higher her labor force participation.
4. The lower the male unemployment rate, the higher the labor force participation rate of married women.
5. The more education a married woman has, the higher her labor force participation. Educational attainment is found to be a particularly important variable in explaining the labor force participation rate of married women.
6. The lower the cost of child care,[c] the higher the labor force participation rate of married women.

---

[c]The cost of child care in 1960 was found to be a very important variable, but we were unable to obtain other than public child care cost data. Therefore, our results cannot be interpreted with precision. But 1970 data on the cost of child care include public and private child care costs.

Supply of Single Women

The labor force participation of single women was also made a function of the median female salary or wage income, educational attainment, and the male unemployment rate. On the basis of regression results, we again obtained some interesting, though not entirely surprising, conclusions, and compare them with those of married women:

1. The higher the female income, the higher the labor force participation of single women. But the labor force participation rate of single women is less sensitive to the income variable than that of married women.
2. The more education a single woman has, the higher her labor force participation. The labor force participation rate of single women is twice as sensitive to educational attainment as that of married women.
3. The lower the male unemployment rate, the higher the labor force participation rate of single women. The labor force participation rate of single women is, however, less sensitive to the male unemployement rate than that of married women.

Demand for Women

In our demand equation the dependent variable, defined as the labor force participation rate of women, was regression on educational attainment, the male unemployment rate, and the expected female employment share. As mentioned earlier, these regression results must be viewed only as tentative and suggestive. However, some interesting conclusions are derived from the demand equation:

1. The more education women have, the higher the labor force participation of women.
2. The higher the male unemployment rate, the lower the labor force participation of women.
3. The higher the expected female employment share, the higher the labor force participation of women.

Regression results obtained from the supply of married women, the supply of single women, and the demand for women are based on cross-sectional decennial census data in 1940, 1950, 1960, and 1970. No time-series data were analyzed. Therefore, one must be careful not to place time-series interpretation on such cross-sectional data. It is of interest to analyze both cross-sectional and time-series data to compare regression results based on the two types of data.

Mincer, Cain, Bowen and Finegan, and Cipriani all have indicated that the income and substitution effects are important theoretical concepts by which the labor force participation of married women with husband present was analyzed. Behind this type of analysis the wife's decision to join the labor force is assumed to be primarily dependent on her husband's social and economic status.

However, this kind of assumption is highly doubtful if the wife's decision to work outside the home is independent of her husband's social and economic status. The family in which two adults are equally able to engage in gainful employment may be interpreted as the two worker family compared with the traditional type of family assumed by Mincer-Cipriani. The two worker family may be interested in maximizing the family income. The family income is more important than each component of the family income. If such is the case, then the income and substitution effects on the supply of wives in the traditional family should be different from those on the supply of wives in the two worker family. If changes in social and economic conditions alter the concept of family from the traditional to the two worker family, as seen developing in Eastern and some Western European countries such as England, Germany, and France,[5] then the assumption underlying the Mincer-Cipriani framework must be highly dubious. Therefore, regression results based on the assumption of the traditional family concept must be viewed as only tentative and suggestive.

Regression results for the period between 1940 and 1970 indicate appreciable changes in the value of the regression coefficients of Y_w, Y_h, and Y_n respectively. A decline in the value of the coefficient of Y_w and a rise in the value of Y_h and Y_n may imply that the positive effect of Y_w is becoming weaker on the labor force participation and that the negative effect of Y_h (or Y_n) is also getting weaker on the labor force participation (Table C of Appendix C). Nevertheless, results show that the maximization of the family income hypothesis was not yet supported for 1970. We suggest that the best possible interpretation based on the 1940-70 results is that while the substitution effect is and will become more attractive to married women with husband present, the maximization of the family income hypothesis is not supported.

Burden of Household Work

We now examine whether the effect of the declining burden of household work on the labor force participation of married women with husband present is significant, or whether the desire for a higher family income provides a better explanation for the increase in the labor force participation of married women.

A popular explanation for the increases in the employment of women, especially that of married women, is the significant reduction in the burden of household work in recent years, due to the increased availability of labor-saving household appliances and time-saving consumer goods and services. A study made by Siegried Giedion describes the development of home mechanization from 1900 to 1940.[6] The earliest improvements involved the introduction of gas in the form of lighting, stoves, and regrigerators. Major gains then came with electricity which made possible electric irons, washing machines, vacuum cleaners, electric stoves, and electric refrigerators all of which contributed further to the decline in the burden of household work.[d]

Although Giedion does not concern himself with the economic returns from home mechanization, Clarence Long has estimated that each dollar's worth of appliances would save one-third hour of household work per year.[7] He has not concluded, however, that household appliances have contributed to increases in the participation of women in the labor force by substituting for household work. He emphasizes, rather, the importance of increased income which is considered to be a key determinant of the participation of women in the labor force.

In an effort to determine whether differences in the possession of household appliances between one worker families (wife not employed) and two worker families (husband and wife employed) are large, we must have information on the ownership of appliances by family income and labor force status of the wife.

Data showing the percentage distribution of three selected household durables (washing machine, washing machine and dryer, and home freezer) by level of family income for two worker families were compared with comparable data for one worker families.[8] In terms of the presence of household durables two sets of data were found to be alike for the same family income categories. Applying the rank-sum test to the data shows that differences in the possession of household appliances between one worker and two worker families are not significant.[e]

More conclusive research must be done before we can arrive at an answer to the question of the importance of the income effect versus the substitution effect. A finer breakdown of data on selected household appliances by family income, size of family, presence or absence of children under 6 years old, employment status of the wife, and so forth would enable us to determine whether the income effect is larger than the substitution effect.

Apart from labor-saving appliances, labor-saving consumer goods such as canned goods, frozen food, partially prepared goods of all types, ready-made clothing, wash and wear clothing, and so forth are substitutes for household work and decrease the burden of housework on women. If data were available, it might show that working women make greater use of these items or, perhaps, greater use of services such as restaurants as an occasional variation on TV dinners than do nonworking women.

---

[d]A brief account of historical development of household appliances is found in the following pages of Giedion's book: the electric and gas stove on page 535; the washing machine on 569; the electric iron on 571-72; the vacuum cleaner on 586-95; and the refrigerator on 602.

[e]The null hypothesis that one worker families are not different from two worker families in the possession of household durables was accepted at the five percent level. For detail see Helen M. Walker and Joseph Lev. *Statistical Inference* (New York: Holt, Rinehart and Winston, 1953), p. 433.

While labor-saving devices have reduced the burden of household work, there are other factors which have contributed to increases in the burden of household work on the woman in higher income households. The decline in the number of household workers per household which has affected higher income families is one of these developments. While changes in the number of household workers does not change the amount of household work which must be performed, a reduction in the number of household workers puts greater burdens on women in the higher income families who might have employed them to free themselves for work outside the home or for other activities. In 1900, for example, there were 99 private household service workers for every 1,000 households. By 1910 this figure had decreased to 91 (Table 6-2). The decline to 58 between 1910 and 1920 was particularly sharp and a result of World War I, which produced higher wages and better working conditions for women in factories and offices and attracted large numbers of domestic household workers. The decline was further encouraged by the decline in the number of immigrants from abroad.

In 1930 the number of domestic household women workers increased to 66.8, reflecting the return to domestic household service of women following the war and the onset of the Depression. The number of household workers per household remained almost constant during the period between 1930 and 1940, but, as in the World War I period, a sharp drop in the number of household workers per household was recorded between 1940 and 1950, the period of World War II. As was the case during World War I, this decline was attributable to the following: (1) a large number of women were attracted to factories as

Table 6-2
Selected Statistics on Domestic and Other Female Workers, 1900-1970

Year	*Domestic Household Workers per 1,000 Households*	*Female Domestic Household Workers (Thousands)*	*Blue-Collar Female Workers*[a] *(Thousands)*	*White-Collar Female Workers*[b] *(Thousands)*
1900	98.9	1,526	1,339	799
1910	91.3	1,784	1,808	1,695
1920	58.0	1,360	1,852	2,857
1930	66.8	1,909	1,976	4,027
1940	69.0	2,277	2,590	5,047
1950	35.9	1,489	3,639	6,993
1960	34.4	1,751	3,881	11,261
1970	27.2	1,627	4,635	18,751

[a]Includes operatives and craftsmen.

[b]Includes nonprofessional white-collar workers.

Sources: Bureau of the Census, *Occupational Trends in the United States, 1900 to 1950,* Table 6; *1960 Census of Population,* Vol. 1, Part 1, U.S. Summary, Table 201; *Current Population Report,* P-60, No. 75, Table 49; *Current Population Report,* P-20, No. 176 and 191; *Historical Statistics of the United States: Colonial Times to 1957,* p. 15.

operatives and clerical and service workers; (2) a continuous rise occurred in the population in suburban areas; and (3) the use of household appliances became more widespread and intensive.

After the war, a large number of women did not return to household service work as they did in the 1920s. This was primarily due to an increase in job opportunities for women in other occupations, in particular, technical, clerical, and service jobs where working conditions and wage and salary income were better than in household work. The number of household workers per household showed a further decline in 1970, reaching the figure of only 27.2 persons per 1,000 households.

Other factors contributing to an increase in the burden of household work were the increase in suburbanization and in home ownership in the post-1940 period since the amount of time required to care for a house and family in a suburban area is more than in the central city.[f] Obviously, a house requires more care than an apartment. Also, it takes more time to drive children to school and to places for social and other activities in suburban areas than in cities. Shopping and running of errands are also likely to take more time.

Still another factor related to higher income brackets is that the wife tends to devote more time to social activity as the husband moves to a higher rank or position in the community. A wife is likely to play an indispensable role in the maintenance and promotion of good relationships with her husband's collegues. Such activity may involve the entertainment of and being entertained by her husband's colleagues either in a business or professional community.

On balance, while we may conclude that the increased availability of household appliances has contributed to a reduction in the burden of household work, countervailing influences have not been a major factor in determining the labor force participation of women. While labor-saving consumer goods and services have also contributed to the decline in the burden of household work, again they have not been a major determinant of the participation of women in the labor force. Despite the increase in these labor-saving devices, the decline in the number of domestic household workers per household and the increase in home ownership in suburban areas have tended to increase the burden of household work, particularly in higher income families.

Recent studies on the burden of household work by housewives[g] indicate

---

[f]The percentage of owner occupied housing units showed continuous increases from 43.6 percent in 1940 to 62.9 percent in 1970 in suburban areas. See *1960 Census of Housing,* Vol. 1, Part 1, U.S. Summary, Table G and *1970 Census of Housing,* Vol. 4, Part 1, Table 2.

[g]Average hours spent on household work per week by all home makers have remained almost unchanged since 1920. The averages were 47.1 hours in 1920, 46.7 hours in 1952, and 47.3 hours in 1968 (P. Nickell and J.M. Dorsey in their book on *Management in Family Living,* New York, Wiley, 1967, p. 127).

While the average hours spent on household work remain almost constant, the presence and age of children, time spent on transportation of persons other than family members,

that more research on home management of working women, concerning the allocation of household chores between husband and wife, must be done. There is a need to determine to what extent an increase in family income attracts married women with husband present into the labor force, while the burden of household work remains almost unchanged over recent decades.

Attitudes toward the Employment of Women

Changing attitudes toward the employment of women which could not be included in our regression equations now merit examination. Our attention will be focused on the extent that such attitudes changed when economic, legal, and other underlying social conditions changed during the past seven decades. In the 1930s, survey data provides more substantial information on attitudes toward the employment of women than Robert Smuts could extract from his survey of literature, court decisions, and reports, comprehensive as these were.[9]

In order to interpret survey data and public opinion polls on attitudes toward the employment of women it is necessary to distinguish between the two ways a respondent feels about the questions on his attitudes. These are: (1) the affective aspect of his attitudes; and (2) the cognitive aspect of his attitudes. By the affective aspect is meant his approval or disapproval, or the intensity of his concern. The cognitive aspect refers to the reasons for his attitudes which may be revealed in his beliefs, values, goals, and knowledge about the employment of women and its effect.

Both the affective and cognitive elements of a person's attitudes toward the employment of married women first became available when public opinion polls began to ask questions on the subject in the mid-1930s. The polls were not concerned with attitudes toward single women working because the employment of single women was common and widely accepted at that time, but the employment of married women was still a public issue with which the pollsters were concerned.

In a 1936 poll by *Fortune* men and women were asked whether married women should have a full time job outside the home. Almost half (48 percent) of the respondents believed that married women should not work.[10] During the 1937-39 period the pollsters were concerned with the affective aspect of attitudes toward whether married women should work if their husbands were capable of supporting them. In 1937 83 percent of the respondents disapproved of married women working. In 1938 the percentage dropped slightly to 78.[11] In 1939 men and women were asked to give their opinions concerning two state

---

and the employment status of wives are important factors affecting hours spent on household work. Average hours spent on household work by employed mothers outside the home, for example, even increased from 4.1 hours in 1952 to 5.3 hours in 1968 under similar working conditions.

legislative proposals which were designed to prohibit married women from working outside the home if their husbands had an income.[12] Apparently still influenced by depression conditions, 67 percent of the respondents approved the bills introduced into the Illinois Legislature while 56 percent approved the Massachusetts bill.

A significant change in attitude toward the employment of married women seems to have occurred during World War II. In 1942 people were asked whether married women should work in war industry. Only 13 percent of the respondents disapproved.[13] But in 1943, when married men were asked how they regarded their own wives working, 55 percent disapproved, suggesting that married men's attitudes—at least toward their own wives—were not significantly changed by the war.[14] Nevertheless, the war appears to have contributed to a change in attitudes. With many men in the armed forces, women were needed in war industries, and the patriotic urge for men and women alike to serve the country was widely felt. When the war ended in 1945, the question of the employment of married women was no longer a burning issue. The 1946 poll once again asked whether married women should work. Only 46 percent of men disapproved, compared with 55 percent in 1943 and 54 percent in 1936.[15]

After 1949 the public opinion polls seem to have lost interest in the subject, considering it no longer controversial. In 1960, however, the University of Michigan Survey Research Center conducted a national survey concerning the employment of married women[16] and found that almost half (48 percent) of the married men still disapproved of wives working outside the home. In 1966, the Department of Labor made a comprehensive survey concerning married women's perception of their husbands' attitudes toward wives working.[17] Again, almost half (48 percent) of the respondents reported that their husbands attitudes were unfavorable.

In summary, attitudes toward married women working were quite stable and negative in the 1930s. They improved dramatically during World War II. But after the war, attitudes appear to have retrogressed yet remained better than in the 1930s. Attitudes in the 1960s showed little change. However, attitudes appear to be improving in the 1970s.[18]

As to the cognitive aspect of attitudes concerning why people disapprove of married women working, more than half of the reasons were related to familial matters while about one-third were concerned that men would lose jobs if women were employed. In 1942 people who disapproved of married women working were asked the reasons for their beliefs. Forty-three percent indicated that women should be in the home while another 43 percent were concerned with the loss of jobs if women were employed. In the Michigan survey, however, 38 percent gave the reason that a woman's place should be in the home, and another 40 percent were concerned with the neglect of children. Thus, familial matters constituted 78 percent of the reasons against wives working.

A recent study by the Manpower Administration of the United States

Department of Labor has attempted to uncover the affective aspect of attitudes toward the participation of married women in the labor force. Selected measures of labor force propensity by tastes for household work, educational attainment, age of children, effect of health, and the husband's attitudes toward his wife's working were examined by asked married women whether they would enter the labor force if they were offered a job.[h]

This study showed that no factor was so significantly associated with the labor force participation of married women as the woman's perception of her husband's attitudes toward her potential employment. Among white women currently out of the labor force, those who regard their husbands' attitudes to be favorable are almost three times as likely to accept a job offer as those who perceive their husbands' attitudes to be unfavorable. In the case of employed women, those who regard their husbands' attitudes to be favorable are more likely to remain in the labor force should they lose their jobs, than those whose husbands have an unfavorable attitude.

It is obvious from these three surveys that a positive attitude of a husband toward his wife's working outside the home, plays an important role in the increase of wives in the labor force. It cannot be determined, however, that the attitude of a husband determines the participation of a wife in the labor force or, on the other hand, is determined by the participation of a wife in the labor force. But it is generally felt that the favorable attitude of husbands toward wives working outside the home encourages wives to seek employment. This tends to increase the participation rate of women in the labor force which could, in turn, affect the attitude of husbands favorably toward the employment of wives.

Federal Laws and Regulations Concerning Sex Discrimination

While economic and social factors were found to be significant in bringing about the increased labor force participation of women, federal laws and regulations concerning sex discrimination have also been effective. They have served both to reinforce the other factors leading to equal treatment of women in the economy and to force their equal treatment when the effect of the other factors has been insufficient to produce the desired result.

No period in history since women acquired the right to vote has demonstrated so serious a concern for the legal status of women as the early 1960s. In 1961 President Kennedy established the President's Commission on the Status of Women, and in 1963, the Civil Service Commission established a policy of equal opportunity for both sexes in federal employment. In the same year the Fair

[h]In the survey 26 percent of married women's husbands did not favor wives working outside the home, while 70 percent favored wives working outside the home.

Labor Standards Act was amended by the Equal Pay Act of 1963 in an attempt to secure equal pay for equal work regardless of sex. Until the enactment of the Civil Rights Act of 1964 "sex" had not been included with race, color, religion, creed, and national origin in federal law or regulations to bar sex discrimination. For the first time a blanket prohibition of discrimination based on sex was added to Title VII of the Civil Rights Act of 1964.

Nevertheless, Title VII of the Civil Rights Act of 1964 is a major piece of legislation, perhaps second only to granting women suffrage in 1920 in securing equal rights for women, but it suffers from limitations in coverage which greatly limit its effectiveness.[i]

The Equal Employment Opportunity Commission (EEOC) rulings require that virtually all jobs must be open to qualified men and women with no regard to stereotyped beliefs and assumptions regarding sex.[j] In short, the applicant must be evaluated on the basis of his or her own individual capabilities. The loose definition of a *bona fide* occupational qualification in section 703 (e) makes it difficult to apply this section in specific instances. Furthermore, the

---

[i]Title VII of the Civil Rights Act of 1964, as initially passed, is applicable only to employers with 25 or more employees, employment agencies referring job applicants to such employers, or labor organizations with 25 or more members. Competitive civil service employees in state and local governments are not covered by Title VII. Administrators and faculty in higher educational institutions are not covered either. Exclusion or exemption of employees in many categories is one of the significant weaknesses of Title VII.

(1) Executive, administrative, and professional employees, including academic administrative personnel and teachers in elementary and secondary schools, and outside sales persons as defined in regulations (29 CFR, Part 541).

(2) Employees of certain retail or service establishments whose annual sales are less than $250,000, and more than 50 percent of whose sales are within the state (hospitals, nursing homes, laundries, dry-cleaners, valet shops, and educational institutions are, however, not exempted. (29 CFR, Part 779).

(3) Employees of certain amusement or recreational establishments, motion picture theaters, small newspapers, and switchboard operators of telephone companies which have fewer than 750 stations (The Equal Pay Act of 1963, Section 13 (a), subsections 3, 8, 9, and 10).

(4) Employees on small farms (29 CFR, Part 780).

(5) Private household workers.

This section states that it is not unlawful to hire an individual on the basis of sex except in certain circumstances when sex is a *bone fide* occupational qualification "necessary to the normal operation of that particular business or enterprise" (*Public Law,* 88-352, Title VII, section 703 (e)).

[j]In 1965 the EEOC issued five guidelines concerning equal employment (*Federal Register,* December 2, 1965, p. 14927). Five guidelines on sex discrimination issued on December, 1965 were superseded and enlarged by the guidelines issued on March 31, 1972. Included are: (1) general principles; (2) sex as a *bone fide* occupational qualification; (3) separate lines of progression and seniority system; (4) discrimination against married women; (5) job opportunities advertising; (6) employment agencies; (7) pre-employment inquiries as to sex; (8) relationship of Title VII to the Equal Pay Act; (9) fringe benefits; (10) employment policies relating to pregnancy and childbirth (see 37 *Federal Register* 6835, April 5, 1972).

EEOC created by Title VII as the administering agency lacks effective enforcing power.[k] Its role is merely informal reconciliation.

After passage of Title VII, many questions arose concerning its relationship to state "protective" laws. In 1969 the EEOC issued guidelines stating that "protective" laws and regulations[l] are in conflict with Title VII, and would not be considered either to protect women or to apply the *bona fide* occupational qualification exception to prospective women workers. In the meantime women fought against discriminatory employment practices in the courts.[m]

An attempt to extend the coverage of the Equal Pay Act of 1963 and of Title VII of the Civil Rights Act of 1964 has resulted in five significant developments which constitute Executive Order 11246 as amended by 11375, the Equal Employment Opportunity Act of 1972, the Education Amendments of 1972, Title IX of the Education Amendments of 1972, and the Comprehensive Health Manpower Act and the Nurse Training Amendments Act of 1971.

The Equal Employment Opportunity Act of 1972 expands coverage of Title VII from employers with 25 or more employees to those with 15 or more

---

[k]Under the cease-and-desist approach a charge is filed with the Commission and the Commission investigates the charge. If reasonable cause is found in the charge, an attempt is made to obtain voluntary compliance. If voluntary compliance is not obtained, the charging party may bring a civil action against the respondent in the federal district court. This approach, according to William Brown III, Chairman, EEOC, is not efficient. The problem that Title VII seeks to correct is to eliminate or reduce sex discrimination in employment as efficiently as possible. As soon as the proof of employment discrimination is completed, relief should be available to charging parties. A mere delay of action due to lack of enforcing power of the EEOC would be of great disservice to aggrieved parties.

For the first seven years between 1964 and 1970, the EEOC was restricted to investigation of discriminatory complaints and voluntary reconciliation. During the 89th Congress Adam Clayton Powell, D-N.Y., introduced a bill that would grant the EEOC the authority to issue cease-and-desist orders enforceable in federal courts, but was not passed despite its endorsement by President Johnson, while civil rights groups and unions had pressed for the EEOC to be given the cease-and-desist power. The Equal Employment Act of 1972 provided the EEOC the court enforcement authority to file suit in federal district courts, an approach favored by the Nixon Administration.

[l]Many states have enacted laws and regulations affecting the employment of women. Some of these laws prohibit the employment of women in certain occupations and restrict women from working as follows: (1) working in mines; (2) working as a bartender; (3) hazardous jobs under certain conditions such as working around coke ovens (Colorado), occupations requiring constant standing (Arizona), working on cores of more than two cubic feet (Massachusetts), handling harmful substances (Michigan), cleaning or working between moving machinery (Missouri), coremaking (New York), and working in blast furnaces, smelters, and quarries, and handling heavy materials of any kind (Ohio); and (4) employment of women before and after child birth. Jobs requiring the lifting and or carrying weight exceeding certain prescribed limits, number of hours per day or per week, and certain hours of night work are restricted.

[m]As for weight-lifting limitations for women see Bowe v. Colgate-Palmolive (416 F.2d 711, 1969). Other cases include the woman's right to work overtime (CCH Employment Practices, 6171 at 4287, 1970), the woman's right to take maternity leave (CCH Employment Practices, 6184 at 4312), and discriminatory hiring practice on the ground that a woman applicant has pre-school age children (400 U.S. 542, 1971).

employees, and from labor organizations with 25 or more members to those with 15 or more members. It also extends coverage to state and local governments, and to nonreligious educational institutions. The 1972 amendments to Title VII add the requirement of nondiscrimination in federal employment. The Civil Service Commission is authorized to enforce antidiscrimination policy and to set up rules and regulations to that effect. While coverage is extended, the Equal Employment Opportunity Act of 1972 authorizes the EEOC to have the power of court action on behalf of victims, if there is reasonable cause in the discrimination charge and if the Commission is unable to secure an informal reconciliation agreement acceptable to the Commission.

Executive Order 11246 as amended by 11375 prohibits sex discrimination in employment (including hiring, upgrading, rates of pay, salaries, fringe benefits, training, layoff, termination, and other conditions of employment) by all contractors and subcontractors with federal contracts of over $10,000. It also requires that affirmative action plans including numerical goals and time tables be implemented by contractors with contracts of $50,000 or more and 50 or more employees. As a result, educational institutions of some size are likely to be covered and required to file affirmative action plans.

Numerical goals are not fixed quotas, but are flexible targets which the contractor attempts to achieve. The aim is affirmative action with the intent of increasing the number of women in the organization of qualified women that are available. But if the contractor fails to meet the goal, it is not considered a violation involving a penalty.

The Equal Pay Act of 1963, amended by the Education Amendments of 1972 extends coverage to executive, administrative, and professional employees, and outside sales persons. All employees in all private and public educational institutions at all levels are covered regardless of whether or not the institution is federally assisted. Affirmative action other than salary increases and back pay is not required to rectify existing pay schedules for both sexes.

Title IX of the Educational Amendments of 1972 prohibits sex discrimination in all federally assisted educational programs.[n] Title IX does not, however, require any affirmative action on the part of educational institutions to rectify disproportional male-female distribution of faculty, staff, and students which may exist. But affirmative action may be required after discrimination is found.

The Comprehensive Manpower Act and the Nurse Training Amendments Act

[n]With regard to admissions to educational institutions Title IX shall apply to institutions of vocational, professional, and graduate education, and public institutions of undergraduate education. Exemptions from the admissions provision are private institutions of undergraduate education, public institutions of undergraduate education of one sex, educational institutions in transition from one sex to coeducation, and elementary and secondary schools other than vocational schools. Other exemptions include religious institutions whose tenets are not consistent with the applicant's qualifications and military schools whose primary purpose is the training of individuals for the military services of the United States or the merchant marine (*Public Law* 92-318, section 901 of Title IX).

of 1971 prohibits sex discrimination in admission of students in all federally assisted institutions in the field of health and medicine. No affirmative action is required to rectify disproportional male-female distributions of students, but may be required if discrimination in admission is found.

In spite of the federal laws and regulations requiring employment in virtually all areas, women do not yet have a legal status equal to that of men. In 1972 the Congress finally adopted the Equal Rights Amendment[o] which would provide a sound legal basis for achieving equal rights for men and women in almost all areas of life: equal admission to public colleges and universities, equal distribution of scholarship funds, equal employment and promotion in public schools, equal pay for equal work, the right to work overtime, the right to establish a business, enter into a contract, manage property, administer an estate, become a guarantor, the right to be drafted into the armed services and receive the same exemptions and deferments as men, the right to serve on a jury and to receive the same penalties as men in violating the laws, etc.

However, the Equal Rights Amendment would not require that sleeping quarters, dormitories, or bathrooms be shared by men and women since the constitutional right of privacy could be used to sanction separate male and female facilities. Furthermore, the Equal Rights Amendment would neither take away the laws for family support nor make alimony unconstitutional, but would require a fairer treatment of men and women on a case by case basis.

There can no longer be any doubt that the EEOC will use the power given it by Congress to take a company or union to court and force it to compensate the women employees it has discriminated against. The $50 million cash settlement worked out in a consent decree on January 18, 1973 by the EEOC and the American Telephone and Telegraph Company (AT & T), the nation's largest employer of women, is a major step forward for women's rights and a warning to other employers. Since the AT & T case, the EEOC has filed some 150 cases against companies such as Mobil Oil, the American Tobacco Company, the Metropolitan Life Insurance Company, General Electric Company, Standard Brands, and General Motors. The EEOC expects to file approximately 600 cases in fiscal 1974, while it has a backlog of thousands of complaints.

The EEOC estimated that women and minorities were subsidizing AT & T to the extent of $500 million a year, or about $3.5 billion since the EEOC was established, through lower pay and underrepresentation in higher paying jobs. Although the settlement fell far short of this figure, Commissioner Brown considered the settlement to be the most significant one in civil rights employment history, and one which illustrates how costly employment discrimination can now be to an employer if effective affirmative action is not taken.

---

[o]As of August, 1973, 30 states have ratified the ERA. Thirty-eight are needed for adoption by March, 1979. For an illuminating discussion of a constitutional basis for equal rights for women, see Barbara A. Brown, Thomas I. Emerson, Gail Falk, and Ann E. Freedman in *Yale Law Journal,* Vol. 80 (April, 1971), pp. 872-985.

The Equal Pay Act of 1963 had covered employees subject to the minimum wage requirements of the Fair Labor Standards Act. But Title IX of the Education Amendments Act of 1972 extended coverage of the Equal Pay Act to an additional 15 million executive, administrative, and professional employees and outside sales persons who had been exempt from coverage. As a result, over 60 of 77 million wage and salary workers are now protected by the Equal Pay Act.

Over 500 cases had been filed by June, 1973 since the Equal Pay Act became effective in June, 1964. The number of employees who had been found underpaid under the Equal Pay Act was over 142,000 through the end of June, 1973, while the amount found due under the Act exceeded $73 million, excluding the cash settlement with AT & T.

"Justified" and "Unjustified" Participation Discrimination

While economic, social, and legal factors have contributed to the rise in the labor force participation of women in the past decades, some women will not be in the labor force for physiological and other reasons. It would therefore be useful to divide the difference in the labor force participation rate of men and women into "invariant" and "variant" components, on the basis of the reasons for nonparticipation. To be consistent with terminology employed in previous chapters, we shall denote "invariant" and "variant" components to be "justified" on the grounds of physiological differences and functions attributable to childbearing and child-rearing, and "unjustified" on the basis of differences in sex roles attributable to social and cultural conditioning. Part of the "unjustified" component could be removed when economic, social, and legal conditions are gradually changed, while the remaining part of the "unjustified" component could not easily be removed even though these conditions are changed. Thus, "unjustified" participation includes both removable and unremovable elements.

To divide the difference between male and female labor force participation into voluntary and involuntary components, we would like to know what proportion of nonparticipants do not want to seek employment and what proportion would be willing and able to work if an opportunity arose. Precise information on these points is hard to come by. However, a 1968 survey of labor force status by sex indicated that five of the seven reasons for nonparticipation given by men and women are of about equal importance (11.3 vs. 10.9 percent). The main reasons for the large male-female difference in participation rates (19.9 vs. 58.4 percent) were differences in concern for retirement benefits (8 vs. 9 percent) and for family responsibilities (.3 vs. 46.7 percent).[19] These findings show that it is concern for family responsibilities directly or indirectly which account for most of the difference in male and female participation rates.

At least three assumptions must be made, therefore, to separate the difference in the participation rate of men and women into "justified" and "unjustified" components:

1. That the proportion of voluntary and involuntary nonparticipants of the entire working age population for reasons other than family responsibilities is the same for men and for women. Consequently, the difference in the labor force participation between men and women is attributable to the family responsibilities of women, or to social and cultural conditioning under which women are led to believe it is proper to stay in the home.

2. That women's nonparticipation for family responsibilities constitutes a temporary withdrawal from the labor force during the childbearing and child-rearing period, or involuntary nonparticipation due to an inability to make proper child care arrangements, or voluntary nonparticipation for a variety of reasons other than childbearing and child-rearing and absence or lack or child care facilities. A recent survey of women's temporary withdrawal from the labor force attributable to childbearing and child-rearing indicates a period between eleven and fifteen months per child, whereas the estimated average working time lost per child by Soviet women is a year's withdrawal from the labor force. If we assume that the time away from work is one full year per child and that on the average men and women would have 40 years of work between 20 and 65, then we could estimate the percentage of total working time lost by women as opposed to men.

In 1970, for example, the number of children born per woman 15 to 44 years old was 1.2. Dividing 1.2 by 40 gives .03, which indicates the percentage of time lost by women (3.0 percent).[p] Results indicate that the percentage of work-loss time by women ranged from 3.0 to 4.4 percent.

3. That one third of women nonparticipants for reasons of family responsibilities indicated that they would be interested in seeking employment if child care arrangements could be made. The remaining two-thirds were not interested in seeking employment.

It is possible to divide the difference in the labor force participation rate between men and women into "justified" and "unjustified" components. Nonparticipation attributable to childbearing and child-rearing for one year per child is justified on physiological grounds. Nonparticipation attributable to the absence of child care facilities is unavoidable and hence justified. Voluntary nonparticipation attributable to reasons other than childbearing and child-rearing and the inability of making proper child care arrangements may also be

[p]The childbearing age of women ranges from 15 to 49, but after age 45 the birth rate drops sharply. Results shown below are based on the number of children ever born per woman 15 to 44 years old, 1900-70. However, no comparable data in 1900 and 1920 were available. It is assumed that the percentage of work loss time by women was 4.0 percent. Percentage of time lost by women during the childbearing and child-rearing period from 1900 to 1970 will be as follows: 4.0 in 1900, 1920, and 1930; 3.0 in 1940; 3.6 in 1950; 4.4 in 1960; and 3.0 in 1970. See Bureau of the Census, *1960 Census of Population,* Vol. 1, Part 1, U.S. Summary, Table 81; *Current Population Report,* P-20, No. 226.

justified, but could be reduced if factors affecting women's beliefs and values concerning proper sex roles in the home and in society could be changed. Thus, it should be considered justified only on a short-term basis.

"Unjustified" nonparticipation in the short-run must, therefore, be involuntary nonparticipation attributable to the absence or lack of job opportunities which discourage or prevent women from joining the labor force. Approximately eight percent of women nonparticipants in 1968 were defined as involuntary nonparticipants.

Table 6-3 presents labor force participation rates of men and women and separates the difference in the labor force participation rate between men and women on nonparticipation grounds into "justified" and "unjustified" components. "Justified" components are: temporary withdrawal from the labor force during the childbearing and child-rearing period; nonparticipation due to the absence or lack of child care facilities; and voluntary nonparticipation primarily due to personal preferences. "Unjustified" nonparticipation is involuntary nonparticipation.

Column 4 of Table 6-3 shows that the nonparticipation rate attributable to childbearing and child-rearing was more or less invariant in the neighborhood of four percent; where column 5, attributable to child care facilities, indicates steady decrease from 21.7 percent in 1900 to 12.1 percent in 1970. Column 6 also shows a continuous decline from 39.4 percent in 1900 to 20.9 percent in 1970, indicating that women's preferences of participation over nonparticipation could be reduced when factors affecting social and cultural conditioning are changed. Column 7 which shows involuntary nonparticipation rate is derived by multiplying the nonparticipation rate of women (100 – column 2) by eight percent. We assume that eight percent of women nonparticipants are involuntary nonparticipants. Column 9 which indicates the voluntary nonparticipation rate is the difference between column 3 and the sum of columns 4 and 7. Column 9 shows a continuous decline from 54.8 percent in 1900 to 28.4 percent in 1970.

The four figures at the beginning of this chapter show graphically the changes which have occurred in the labor force participation of women over the past half century. The influence of demographic factors—changes in the age composition and age-marital status of the female population—played an insignificant role in causing these changes. Indeed their effect, taken alone, was slightly negative. More important in bringing about the increased participation of women in the labor force are factors revealed by our regression analysis of the demand for and supply of women. The increased educational attainment of women and the increased employment opportunities for them were found to be particularly important in explaining the increase.

Another factor which is not amenable to regression analysis, but which is considered to be of major importance in explaining the increase in participation, is the change in the public's attitude toward women working, particularly married women, which has occurred since the 1930s. Public opinion polls also

Table 6-3
Labor Force Participation Rates and "Justified" and "Unjustified" Nonparticipation Rates, 1900-1970

Year	*Men (1)*	*Women (2)*	*Differ-ence (3)*[a]	*Child Birth (4)*[b]	*Child Care (5)*[c]	*Other Home Respon-sibility (6)*[d]	*Involuntary or "Unjusti-fied" Nonpar-ticipation (7)*[e]	*"Justified" Nonparti-cipation (8)*[f]	*Voluntary Nonparti-cipation (9)*[g]
1900	85.7	20.6	65.1	4.0	21.7	39.4	6.3	58.8	54.8
1920	84.6	22.7	61.9	4.0	20.6	37.3	6.1	55.8	51.8
1930	82.1	23.6	58.5	4.0	19.5	35.0	6.1	52.4	48.4
1940	79.7	25.7	54.0	3.0	18.0	33.0	5.9	48.1	45.1
1950	79.0	29.0	50.0	3.6	16.6	29.8	5.6	44.4	40.8
1960	82.4	37.1	45.3	4.4	15.1	25.8	5.0	40.3	35.9
1970	79.2	42.8	36.4	3.0	12.1	21.3	4.6	31.8	28.8

[a]Column 3 = col. 1 – col. 2 = col. 4 + col. 5 + col. 6.

[b]Column 4 = see footnote p, p. 92.

[c]Column 5 = col. 3/ 3 is assumed, based on the 1968 BLS survey.

[d]Column 6 = col. 3 – (col. 4 + col. 5).

[e]Column 7 = .08 (100 – col. 2), based on the 1968 BLS survey.

[f]Column 8 = col. 3 – col. 7.

[g]Column 9 = col. 8 – col. 4.

Sources: Bureau of the Census, *Occupational Trends in the United States 1900-1950,* Tables 6a and 6b; *1960 Census of Population,* Vol. 1, Part 1, U.S. Summary, Table 81; *Current Population Report,* P-20, No. 226; Bureau of Labor Statistics, *Special Labor Report,* No. 119.

indicate that World War II caused a significant positive change in the public's attitutde toward married women working. By the end of the war, the issue of married women working had become noncontroversial. More recent polls have indicated, however, a continuing undercurrent of male disapproval of married women working, particularly on the part of husbands when asked about their own wives. Nevertheless, working wives appear to be receiving more approbation and support than was the case earlier, and this appears to be a significant factor in explaining the greater participation of married women in recent years. Also, legislation supporting the principle of equal rights and equal treatment, has unquestionably had a positive effect on female participation in the past half dozen years.

Household work seems to follow Parkinson's law in the sense that as improvements in household technology are made, the work expands to fill all the available time of the homemaker. Beyond this, the number of domestic workers per household has shrunk drastically over past decades. As a result, the factors working toward freeing women from household chores for work outside the home have largely been counteracted by other developments.

Since the participation of single women in the labor force is already quite high in relation to that of men for all age groups, there is little room for further increase. The participation of married women with husband absent has increased significantly in recent decades, particularly in the older age groups when children are in school or grown up. From the late twenties to the early fifties the rate is between 65 and 70 percent. Therefore, in these ages, room for improvement is not large, but there is hope for significant increases in labor force participation in the ages between the early twenties and late thirties.

Our discussion suggests it is not discrimination in the narrow sense of unfair or unequal treatment by employers which can change this, but reduction in the burden of bearing and rearing children and of housework generally, further improvement in the attitude of husbands toward their wives working, and a more positive attitude toward women with families working. Findings among Soviet and European women, as well as among dual career families here, suggest that many married women find that family life benefits from the wife and mother being actively engaged in a career which provides satisfactions, greater varieties of experiences, more self confidence, and other benefits. Married women who work have often found that they can do so at little or no expense to family life. Indeed, they may find that they are more fulfilled and better wives and mothers as a consequence.

In concluding this chapter, we shall briefly indicate two areas for further research which are considered to be significant.

1. A more meaningful explanation of the supply of women could be made by utilizing cross-sectional and time-series data. The maximization of family income hypothesis and the life cycle hypothesis would be worth investigation in the context of the income and substitution effects.

2. Our estimate of the demand for women is far from satisfactory in the absence of relevant data on the demand side. Furthermore, the demand equation fails to make a distinction between the increase in demand for women attributable to changes in hiring practices, or the increase in the demand for women attributable to changes in women's qualifications. It is more meaningful to determine the type of the demand equation based on women of equivalent qualifications, measured by level of educational attainment, work experience, and other relevant characteristics. In accomplishing this objective, the development of qualitative data on men and women workers by detailed occupation, educational attainment, and work experience is required. The male and female equations would then be compared for SMSAs or regions.

7 Summary and Conclusions

This study began with a definition of economic discrimination against women. Our point of departure was the concept of total discrimination which we measured by the difference between total male and female earnings in the economy as a whole or, in some instances, by the difference in male and female earnings in selected occupational groups. Thus, if there were no differences in the participation rates of men and women, or in their employment in the various occupations, or in their rates of pay for doing the same work, total income from earnings of men and women, for all practical purposes, would be equal, and there would be no evidence of discrimination. We started from this extreme point of departure, not in the belief that women will ever wish to work in precisely the same jobs or for the same portion of their lives or with the same intensity as men. Rather, we feel that it provides a useful base line, any departure from which can be measured and examined to determine the cause and the extent to which the departure is justified in economic terms in either the short or the long run.

Our approach to the analysis of discrimination can be seen schematically in Figure 7-1. This diagram is an oversimplification, but its simplicity helps clarify the assumptions upon which our analysis was based and the framework employed in this study. The first column shows the various sources of the male-female earnings differential. That part of the differential due to physiological (and possibly psychological) differences which are permanent must, therefore, be considered as representing justified discrimination against women. An example of this would be the reduced earnings of a woman due to time lost in childbirth.

The part of the differential due to social and cultural conditioning which has an adverse effect on developing female capabilities cannot be eliminated quickly. An example of this form of culturally imposed discrimination would be the failure of more women to seek training in high income occupations such as management, law, engineering, and medicine. Such sex role conditioning affecting women's preferred choice of occupations may take a generation or more to change. Therefore, the failure of an employer to hire as many female as male civil engineers must be considered to represent temporarily justified discrimination. A related type of temporarily justified discrimination is the preference of some women not to work at all. We view this self-imposed discrimination as conditioned by the social and cultural environment at a given time in a given society. It represents, therefore, in the terms of our analysis, a

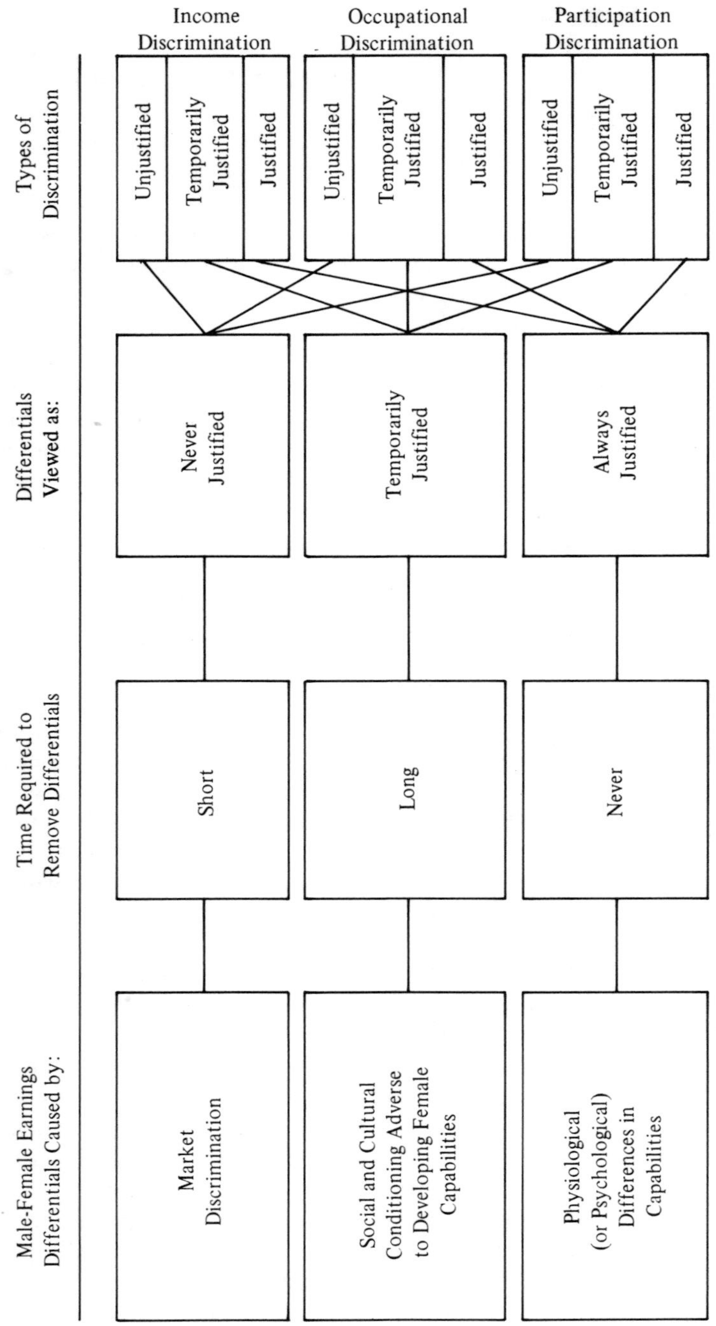

Figure 7-1. Causes of Earnings Differentials and Types of Discrimination.

form of temporarily justified discrimination which will gradually disappear as complete equality between men and women is approached, particularly in the realm of work and domestic responsiblities.

The part of the differential in male-female earnings due to market discrimination usually can be removed in a rather short time by changes in hiring policy, even if not in attitude, by employers. If past market discrimination which prevented women from gaining experience in a particular kind of job needed for advancement is involved, it may take a considerable amount of time to eliminate earnings differences even after the barriers to advancement are removed. Women must have the time necessary to gain the prior experience needed.

The difference between male and female earnings can be divided into three types of discrimination which are responsible for the gap: income discrimination, occupational discrimination, and participation discrimination. As indicated in Figure 7-1, each of these components can be further divided into the parts caused by unjustified, temporarily justified, and justified discrimination. Drawing on our previous illustration, the small number of women employed as civil engineers would be an example of temporarily justified occupational discrimination. Only as more women became trained as civil engineers could employers properly be expected to employ a higher proportion of women engineers. Only then, if the proportion of women failed to increase, would unjustified occupational discrimination be considered to exist.

The purpose of this scheme of analysis outlined in Figure 7-1 is to help clarify the factors which have caused changes in the three components of total discrimination and to help identify the factors which are most in need of change if women's total earnings are to be brought closer to those of men.

Of course, total earnings of men and women differ and differ substantially. But significant changes in the relationship have occurred over recent decades. We found that total discrimination in the economy as a whole decreased by 8 percentage points between 1940 and 1970. There was an initial decline of 5 percentage points between 1940 and 1950 as a result of the favorable impact of World War II, followed by a slight increase of 2 percentage points between 1950 and 1960, reflecting a retrogression in income and occupational discrimination. This setback was followed by a decrease in discrimination of 5 percentage points in the 1960s, a decrease based on an overall improvement in the situation of working women. Further decreases are now in process.

When we examined by the use of index numbers changes in the three components of total discrimination—income discrimination, occupational discrimination, and participation discrimination—we found developments in certain of these three components at odds with the changes in total discrimination.

First, the index of income discrimination in the economy as a whole increased surprisingly by almost 5 percentage points during the period between 1940 and 1970. Although decreases occurred in the periods from 1940 to 1950 and from 1960 to 1970 (the periods favorably affected by World War II and the Equal Pay Act), the increase in discrimination during the 1950s still outweighed them. During that decade each of the five occupational groups also showed an increase in income discrimination, an increase ranging from 3.4 to 22.9 percentage points.

During the 1940 to 1970 period, occupational discrimination for full time year-round workers at first decreased sharply in the 1940s, then gradually increased in the 1950s and 1960s to a 1970 level which was 13 percent below the 1940 level. The 1940s were a wartime period in which many women entered occupations normally dominated by men. However, the proportion of women in the traditional sales, clerical, and service jobs also increased at this time. Following the war, returning service men largely replaced the women who had entered the traditional male occupations, many of which were relatively highly paid ones. As a result, occupational discrimination increased from 1950 to 1960, in part because manpower shortages were alleviated and the economy operated below full employment levels. Occupational discrimination decreased again in the more prosperous 1960s, reflecting not only fuller employment but also the blanket prohibition of sex discrimination in hiring under Title VII of the Civil Rights Act of 1964. In addition, the proportion of women in most major occupational groups increased, particularly in the managerial, sales, and craftsmen groups, although the proportion of women operatives decreased.

Over the entire period from 1900 to 1970, there was a slight increase in occupational discrimination for the all worker category. The index first decreased in the period from 1900 to 1920, but then increased steadily from 1920 to 1970.

Participation discrimination against women workers showed a remarkable decline over the seven decades between 1900 and 1970, evident in the striking increases in the participation rate from 21 to 43 percent. This doubling in the rate was the result of significant changes in the participation of married women of all ages, but particularly in the older age groups. Married women, beginning with World War II, increasingly reentered the labor force after the childbearing and child-rearing years. The participation of single women, on the other hand, which has always been high, did not change nearly as dramatically over this period. Indeed, with the participation rate of married women now high, except during the childbearing and child-rearing years, and that of married women with husband absent and single women even higher, the room for further increases in the overall participation rate of women has been much reduced. Nonetheless, the rate for women sixteen years and over has reached only 43 percent, while that of men is 80 percent. Therefore, the remaining room for progress is substantial.

Turning to specific occupations, we found that participation discrimination has decreased moderately in clerical and sales occupations, the percentages passing the fifty-fifty ratio in the 1920s for the former and in the 1970s for the latter. Thus, both these occupations are now dominated by women. There was also a significant sharp decline in participation discrimination in managerial occupations and a small decline for professional, farm, blue-collar, and unskilled workers. Participation discrimination in private household work, an area completely dominated by women, remained virtually unchanged during the same period.

In other more limited areas, the trends in participation discrimination were varied. In the field of higher education, participation discrimination declined between 1960 and 1965 for instructors. Participation discrimination remained close to zero in the combined field of elementary and secondary education during the 1950-60 period, but surprisingly, men now make up more than half of the employment in this field. In the health profession, a small increase in the proportion of men indicated that participation discrimination decreased between 1950 and 1960, for as we defined participation discrimination, a decrease in the proportion of women in a profession with an excess of women represents a decrease in participation discrimination, i.e., a move toward a fifty-fifty ratio of men and women.

In federal employment, participation discrimination among professionals was much greater than among nonprofessionals where the proportion of men and women employed in 1968 was nearly equal. In addition, participation discrimination among professionals increased between 1959 and 1968, while it decreased for nonprofessionals. Since the latter group represents a much larger number of employees, participation discrimination for all federal employees decreased during the 1959-68 period.

After examining trends in total discrimination and in each of its components, we attempted in the second part of this study to determine the factors affecting changes in each of the components of discrimination which had been measured–income discrimination, occupational discrimination, and participation discrimination.

The earnings differential between men and women doing the same work was explained by a number of factors, some economically justified, others not. We attempted to divide the earnings differential between men and women into economically "justified" and "unjustified" components on the basis of productivity differences.

Productivity differences between men and women in office and factory work were found to be marginal, differing by no more than five percentage points. Therefore, differences in pay in these jobs would be difficult to justify on economic grounds. In academic fields, by contrast, our findings indicated that the scholarly productivity of women in 1970 was less than half that of men. Therefore, on the surface, salary differentials would seem to be justified in these fields. However, if the burden of housework were more equally shared and other inequalities removed, the scholarly or scientific productivity of women would undoubtedly be much higher and substantially reduce the proportion of the differential which could be justified.

Male-female differences in nonwage costs, such as absenteeism and labor turnover, were found to be small. The largest male-female difference was among operatives, but even here the difference in the proportion of lost earnings to total possible earnings due to absenteeism caused by sickness was only 1.3 percentage points in favor of men. All other occupational groups had smaller male-female differences in the cost of absenteeism.

The cost of labor turnover to the employer was higher for women than for men, but the difference in the expected average cost of this turnover was no more than $40 for the blue-collar, clerical, and sales-service groups. However, the difference for professionals was $276, a figure high enough to have some influence upon hiring practices.

We next divided the earnings differential between men and women into components attributable to differences in hours worked, educational attainment, job seniority, and absenteeism. An unexplained residual remained due to factors whose effect could not be measured individually.

The effect of each of the four factors was estimated by the additional earnings that women would have earned had there been no differences between men and women in hours worked, educational attainment, job seniority, and absenteeism. Such additional earnings for all occupations in 1970 were $575, $360, $360, and $8, respectively, for the differences in hours worked, educational attainment, job seniority, and absenteeism. The share of all these additional earnings in the differential between men and women varied considerably among the occupational groups, ranging from 16 to 33 percent in 1950, from 19 to 49 percent in 1960, and from 5 to 37 percent in 1970.

We then divided, on economic grounds, the earnings differential between men and women into "justified" and "unjustified" components. The "justified" component was the sum of differences attributable to hours worked, educational attainment, job seniority, and absenteeism. The "unjustified" component was the difference between the earnings differential and the "justified" component.

It is difficult to determine the "unjustified" components since the broad occupational categories employed by the census, despite a breakdown into some 300 occupations, obscure the fact that within a given occupation men and women often are doing quite different work and have quite different levels of productivity, justifying different levels of pay. The narrower definition of occupation by the Bureau of Labor Statistics enabled us to analyze somewhat more accurately the economically justifiable earnings differential between men and women that was attributed to differences in the actual work performed.

For a precise determination of the "unjustified" component of the earnings differential between men and women, one must turn to the courts. Only when individual and specific cases are examined, as is done by the courts, is it possible to determine whether the work performed is in fact equal and whether differences in pay are justified by differences in the work performed. These cases suggest that income discrimination is in fact less than the general statistical measures show. As a result, they raise some doubt as to the validity of the more general statistical measures of the census and BLS and suggest that further improvements through more precise and coordinated census and BLS data are necessary.

Occupational discrimination which results in women being underrepresented in the higher paying occupations and overrepresented in the lower paying ones is a consequence of discrimination in hiring and of social and cultural conditioning or sex role socialization which inhibits women's aspirations and prevents women from developing interests in and capabilities for pursuing and succeeding in certain lines of work. Our results indicate that discrimination based on social and cultural conditioning is substantial in the male-dominated occupations such as medicine, law, and engineering. Historically, American women have been discouraged from even considering these fields as appropriate for them. The overrepresentation of women in the female-dominated occupations such as nursing and secretarial work is also to a large degree attributable to the social and cultural conditioning of males as well as females which leads men to avoid these traditionally female fields.

Discrimination in hiring may be justified in the short-run on the grounds that too few women have been trained or are looking for work in insufficient numbers to make the employment of as many women as men possible. Therefore, we separated hiring discrimination into "justified" and "unjustified" components based on the numbers of women presently trained. Our findings show that in twenty major professional fields "unjustified" discrimination in hiring is substantial in sociology, history, engineering, mathematics, and chemistry. The least discrimination was found in the fields of computer science, dentistry, medicine, law, and nursing. Here almost all women who are trained are employed. In several of these fields the problem is that too few women obtain the required training.

Some women may choose not to take jobs for which they have been trained or, indeed, to take any job at all. Such self-imposed discrimination, which is largely attributable to inhibiting social and cultural conditioning, appears to be unavoidable in the short run, but it can be reduced or removed in the long run by conscientious efforts to encourage young women to develop their potential in all fields of specialization, including the traditionally male fields.

Practical ways in which discrimination in hiring can be removed were indicated in the last section of Chapter 5. These include a more equal sharing of family burdens between husband and wife, changed work regimes to accomodate women, more energetic legal action, etc. These methods are now being encouraged by the government and by various private agencies and organizations.

Participation in the labor force and changes in the participation rate depend on a number of factors. We found demographic factors such as age composition and age-marital status to be insignificant in explaining the long-term rise in the participation rate of women in the post-1940 period. Indeed, the effect they had was negative. Other factors, therefore, had to be responsible for the increased participation rate.

We next examined demand and supply factors with the aid of regression equations. Educational attainment and employment opportunity were found to be the two most important factors in explaining the rise in the participation rate. In addition, the increasingly favorable attitude of husbands toward wives working outside the home played an important role in explaining increases in the participation rate of women.

While the availability of labor-saving household appliances and time-saving consumer goods and services has contributed to reducing the burden of household work, the positive effects have been at least partially negated by the decrease in the number of domestic service workers per household. Also, increases in home ownership in suburban areas have contributed to an increase in the burden of household work for women, particularly in higher income families. Indeed, as a result of these contradictory developments, the effect of the burden of household work on the long-term participation rate of women, particularly married women, has remained fairly constant.

Using as a basis the various Bureau of Labor Statistic surveys of nonworking women, we separated the difference in the participation rate between men and women into "justified" and "unjustified" components. The part of the difference which is primarily attributable to women's family responsibilities such as childbirth and child care constitutes the hard core of nonparticipation on "justified" grounds. At a given time, however, the preferences of women for homemaking are considered to constitute nonparticipation on "justified" grounds as well. Nonparticipation on "unjustified" grounds is, therefore, that part of the difference due to the lack of job opportunities for women. Over the seven decades between 1900 and 1970 "unjustified" or involuntary nonparticipation showed a slight decline from 6.4 percent in 1900 to 4.6 percent in 1970, while "justified" nonparticipation showed a remarkable decline from 59 percent in 1900 to 32 percent in 1970. These seven decades were a period during which social, cultural, economic, and legal factors adversely affecting the participation of women in the labor force were being drastically reduced or eliminated. However, the improvement in female participation reflects, of course, not only a lowering of many barriers but also a rise in the desire of women to participate actively in the labor force as their conception of themselves and their role changed. With the interaction of these phenomena, much of the nonparticipation which would have seemed justified to most women at the turn of the century became unjustified and was replaced with active and, for most women, rewarding participation.

While there has been some progress in recent years toward the reduction of discrimination against women in the economy as a whole and in the particular professional groups we examined, discrimination against women is still the rule rather than the exception. Factors adversely affecting women in pay, in occupation, and in participation are deep-seated. Stereotyped notions about the undesirability of women working, prejudice against women's capability in traditional male fields, and differences between the processes of socialization in the family and in society for boys and girls are all deeply embedded in our society and culture. These are all elements of a pervasive conservatism in the human condition which resists change. As a consequence, social and cultural conditioning which supports income differentials will change only gradually unless special efforts to encourage or reinforce change are made.

A more rapid resolution of the problem of discrimination calls for positive attitudes toward women's capabilities in all fields and the provision of working conditions and social services adjusted to the life cycle of women. It is not enough, however, to change the role played by women, The roles of both men and women must change. If complete equality is to be achieved, the division of functions between the sexes must be altered so that men play a more equal and active role both as husbands and parents. The husband's traditional role as provider must be modified to permit a shared responsibility for the support and care of children. We believe that neither a decisive nor a lasting improvement in the position of women is possible as long as women are not economically independent in marriage and men fail to share more fully in household work. Otherwise, the woman's work will always take second place to her husband's and suffer as a consequence. The dual career family with an equal sharing of household burdens and responsibilities must become the accepted norm.[1]

The reduction or removal of the remaining barriers to the full realization of women's equality requires conscientious efforts to this end on the part of men and women, the various organizations and groups concerned with women's rights, our educational system at all levels, and the relevant government agencies working toward equality through legal, social, and economic means.

Appendix A
Method of Making Article Counts

In 1970 approximately 313,000 of 377,000 potentially qualified scientists were included in the *National Register* of the National Science Foundation. The term "qualified" varies among the different fields of science. For example, the American Chemical Society considers a person who has a bachelor's degree in chemistry and is employed in a position requiring a knowledge of chemistry to be a qualified chemist, while experimental biologists must have the M.D. or Ph.D. degree and have several years of research experience. The eligibility criteria based on academic training and work experience are, therefore, determined by the respective scientific professional societies. The National Science Foundation accepts suggestions and recommendations from the respective professional societies on the eligibility criteria.

The following fourteen fields were taken from the *National Register of Scientific and Technical Personnel 1970,* Table A-59 and the remaining six fields from the Bureau of Labor Statistics estimate of women professionals, *College Graduated Workers, 1968-80:*

National Register of National Science Foundation	*Bureau of Labor Statistics*
Mathematics	Engineering
Statistics	Education
Computer Science	American History
Physics	Law
Atmospheric Sciences	Literature
Earth Sciences	Theater (plays)
Chemistry	
Biological Sciences	
Anthropology	
Economics	
Political Science	
Psychology	
Linguistics	
Sociology	

Method of Counts

Some articles were published by male and female scientists. If an article bears both male and female names, the article is counted one half. If however, an article bears one male (female) and two or more females (males), the article is counted as one by women (men).

The following journals were suggested by librarians and professionals as significant and representative in each field. Unfortunately certain journals which would otherwise be selected could not be used because only the initials of the authors' first names were used.

Field	*Professional Journal*
Mathematics	*Mathematical Review,* January, April, July and October, 1970
Statistics	*Journal of the American Statistical Association,* 1969-70
Computer Science	*Journal of the Association for Computing Machinery,* 1968-70
Physics	*Physical Review,* Part A, January-April, 1970; Part B, January-February, 1970; Part C, January-June, 1970
Atmospheric Science	*Meteorological and Geoastrophysical Abstracts* January, 1970
Earth Sciences	*U.S. Geophysical Abstracts,* January-April, 1970
Chemistry	*Journal of Inorganic and Nuclear Chemistry* 1970-71; *Microchemical Journal,* 1970-71; *Journal of Physiology,* 1970-71
Biological Sciences	*Journal of Theoretical Biology,* 1969-70; *Journal of Molecular Biology,* 1969-70; *Journal of Experimental Biology,* 1969-70
Engineering	*Journal of the American Society of Mechanical Engineering,* Sections A through F, 1970
Anthropology	*American Anthropologist,* 1966-70; *American Journal of Physical Anthropology,* 1966-70; *Southwestern Journal of Anthropology,* 1966-70
Economics	*American Economic Review,* 1970; *Journal of Political Economy,* 1970; *Quarterly Journal of Economics,* 1970; *Review of Economics and Statistics,* 1970; *Review of Economic Studies,* 1970; *Journal of Economic Theory,* 1970
Political Science	*Politics,* 1966-70; *Political Science Quarterly,* 1966-70; *American Academy of Political and Social Science,* 1966-70; *Western Political Quarterly,* 1966-70; *Review of Politics,* 1966-70; *American Political Science Review,* 1966-70; *Journal of Politics,* 1966-70
Psychology	*Psychological Abstracts,* January-June, 1970
Sociology	*Sociological Abstracts,* 1970
English and Drama	*1969 MLA International Bibliography of Books and Articles on the Modern Languages,* Vol. 1, *Plays in Periodicals 1900-68 in 97 Periodicals*
American History	*American History and Life,* 1970
Linguistics	*1969 MLA International Bibliography of Books and Articles,* Vol. 3
Education	*Journal of Educational Research,* 1966-70; *Journal of Education,* 1966-70; *History of Education Quarterly,* 1966-70;

Field	*Professional Journal*
	Journal of Higher Education, 1966-70; *High School Journal,* 1966-70; *Elementary School Journal,* 1966-70; *Harvard Education Review,* 1966-70; *Educational Record,* 1966-70
Law	*University of Chicago Law Review,* 1968-70; *Annual Survey of American Law,* 1968-70; *Wisconsin Law Review,* 1968-70; *Harvard Law Review,* 1968-70; *Law and Society Review,* 1968-70; *Northwestern University Law Review,* 1968-70; *Michigan Law Review,* 1968-70; *Columbia Law Review,* 1968-70; *Georgetown Law Review,* 1968-70

Appendix B
Labor Force Participation Rates of Women by Age and Marital Status in Selected Years

Table B-1
Labor Force Participation Rates of Women by Age, 1900-1970

Age	*1900*	*1920*	*1940*	*1950*	*1960*	*1970*
Total, 14 years and older	20.0	23.7[a]	25.8	29.0	34.5	42.6[c]
14-19 years	26.8	32.7[b]	18.9	22.6	23.8	39.4[d]
20-24	31.7	38.1	45.6	43.2	44.8	56.9
25-29	19.4	22.4	35.5	32.6	35.1	45.8
30-34			30.9	30.9	35.5	45.0
35-39	15.0		28.3	33.9	40.2	51.0
40-44			26.0	36.2	45.3	
45-49	14.2	18.0	23.7	34.8	47.4	54.0
50-54			21.2	30.8	45.8	
55-59	12.6		18.5	25.9	39.7	49.1
60-64		9.0	14.8	20.5	29.5	36.4
65 years and over	8.3		6.1	7.8	10.3	9.8

[a]15 years and older.
[b]15-19 years.
[c]16 years and older.
[d]16-19 years.

Sources: Gertrude Bancroft, *The American Labor Force* (New York: Wiley, 1958), Table D; Bureau of the Census, *1920 Census of Population,* Vol. 4, Chapter 6, Table 5; *1960 Census of Population,* Vol. 1, Part 1, U.S. Summary, Table 195; Bureau of Labor Statistics, *Special Labor Force Report,* No. 130, Table A.

Table B-2
Labor Force Participation Rates of Women by Age and Marital Status, 1940-70

Age and Marital Status	*1940*	*1950*	*1960*	*1970*
Married, husband present				
Total, 14 years and older	13.8	21.6	30.6	40.8[a]
14 to 19	9.3	19.4	26.0	36.0[b]
20 to 24	17.3	26.0	31.1	47.4
25 to 29	18.5	22.1	26.8	38.4
30 to 34	17.6	22.5	29.0	40.2
35 to 44	15.3	26.5	36.5	47.2
45 to 54	11.1	23.0	39.3	49.5
55 to 64	7.1	13.1	25.2	32.4
65 and older	2.8	4.5	6.8	7.9

Table B-2 continued

Age and Marital Status	*1940*	*1950*	*1960*	*1970*
Single women				
Total, 14 years and older	45.5	46.3	42.9	53.0[a]
14 to 19	19.7	22.8	23.3	39.5
20 to 24	73.1	73.3	73.2	71.1
25 to 29	79.5	79.8	79.1	82.5
30 to 34	77.7	77.9	79.4	77.2
35 to 44	73.4	75.7	78.2	73.3
45 to 54	63.5	70.7	76.1	72.3
55 to 64	47.2	57.2	64.8	63.7
65 and older	16.9	19.7	23.0	17.6
All other-ever-married women[c]				
Total, 14 years and older	33.7	35.5	38.7	39.1[a]
14 to 19	34.6	37.0	35.3	46.9[b]
20 to 24	57.0	54.3	53.9	59.7
25 to 29	63.9	59.3	58.2	66.0
30 to 34	66.6	62.4	62.2	64.0
35 to 44	61.9	65.7	68.2	67.9
45 to 54	46.6	56.2	67.3	69.1
55 to 64	26.8	35.8	47.6	54.6
65 and older	6.2	7.8	10.6	9.9

[a]16 years and older.

[b]16 to 19 years.

[c]Includes widowed, divorced, and married women with husband absent.

Sources: Bureau of the Census, *1960 Census of Population,* Vol. 2, Part 6-A, Table 6; Bureau of Labor Statistics, *Special Labor Force Report,* No. 130, Table A.

Appendix C
Regression Analysis: The Supply of Married Women, Single Women; The Demand for Women

Criteria for Inclusion of Selected Variables[a]

This is a cross-sectional study based on decennial census data in 1940, 1950, 1960, and 1970. No attempt was made to analyze time series data of the labor force participation of women.[b]

Husband's Income and Wife's Income

Cross-sectional studies on the labor force participation of married women with husband present have shown that the lower a husband's income, the higher the labor force participation of a married woman. The inverse relationship between the husband's income and the labor force participation of the wife is partially offset, however, by the positive relationship between the wife's income and her labor force participation.

Jacob Mincer explains the increase in the labor force participation of married women by indicating that the substitution effect is stronger than the income effect.[1] Glen Cain, William G. Bowen and T.A. Finegan, and Corindo Cipriani all[2] have confirmed the income effect and substitution effect on the supply of married women in Mincer's framework.

Nonlabor Income

Nonlabor income, defined as additional income received by the family such as dividends, interest, and other miscellaneous income derived from property and financial transactions, is interpreted in the same way as the husband's income. Thus, nonlabor income is expected to be negative in sign. Results shown by Cain, Bowen and Finegan, and Cipriani all confirmed the income effect of nonlabor income on the supply of married women.

Educational Attainment

Educational attainment is positively associated with the labor force participation

[a]For a brief discussion of variables used in regressions see Note 1.

[b]Time series data of the labor force participation of women are available on tape from the

of women. One interpretation is that the more education a woman has, the more expensive the opportunity cost of not being in the labor force. Hence she is more likely to be in the labor force, substituting market work for home work. If the acquisition of education is a type of investment in human capital, then it appears to be reasonable to interpret education as a taste for market work. Mincer, Cain, Bowen and Finegan, and Cipriani all included educational attainment as an independent variable seeking to explain the labor force participation rate of married women.

Male Unemployment Rate

The male unemployment rate is intended to measure general economic conditions which affect the participation of women in the labor force. But this variable does not necessarily reflect general economic conditions. The degree of capacity utilization is a better measure of general economic conditions than the male unemployment rate. In the absence of data on capacity utilization in each SMSA, however, we must make use of the male unemployment rate as a proxy of economic conditions.

The female unemployment rate, though highly correlated with the male unemployment rate, was not employed in regression equations because it is not a good measure of economic facts in each SMSA. Further, the female unemployment rate is correlated with the extent of the labor force participation of women. Therefore, it is not valid to use the female unemployment rate as an independent variable in a regression seeking to explain the participation rate of women in the labor force.

Child Care Cost

The labor force participation rate of married women with husband present and with one child or more under 6 years of age is lower than that of married women with husband and without children. Mincer, Cain, Bowen and Finegan, and Cipriani all included in their equations the presence of children, measured by the proportion of married women who have one child or more under 6 years of age, and interpreted this variable as the family taste for home work.

The cost of child care is a more useful measure than the variable employed by Mincer-Cipriani because it is possible to measure the direct economic effect of the cost of child care on the participation of married women in the labor force (for a detailed discussion see Note 2).

Bureau of the Census. In the absence of financial support, however, no data tapes were employed either in part or in full in this study.

Employment Opportunities

Empirical work on the demand for women is relatively scarce compared with that on the supply of married women. Some writers point out important variables in explaining the demand for married women. As one of the demand factors, employment opportunities of women may be important in the determination of the demand equation. John Durand, for example, recognizes the demand factors favorable to the increase in employment of women. Those factors which are favorable to women include the increase in demand for white-collar and professional workers, and the substitution of female for male workers in certain occupations, in particular, in tobacco manufacturing, or mechanics and welders during World War II.[3]

Cain introduces to his regression equations a variable defined as the proportion of male workers that are employed by male dominated industries.[4] Industries such as mining, construction, agriculture, transportation, communication, and durable manufacturing employ more male workers than female workers, whereas personal services, hospitals, and some retail stores employ more female workers than male workers. The proportion of male workers in an area was then used as a proxy of the demand for male workers. When this variable is used as an independent variable in explaining the participation rates of married women in the labor force, the sign of the variable is expected to be negative.

The most carefully constructed variable as a proxy of the demand for women for each SMSA is the one by Bowen and Finegan.[5] This variable was constructed on the basis of the expected female employment share in each SMSA. The observed female employment share is not valid because it is correlated with the extent of the participation rate of women in the labor force. But the expected female employment share is a valid measure, though not entirely a preferred one.

We estimated our version of the expected female employment share as a proxy of the demand for women in each SMSA (see Note 3).

Supply of Married Women

The supply of married women with husband present is analyzed based on the following assumptions:

1. The two adults in a family are equally able to engage in gainful employment if they so desire.
2. The family income is the sum of the husband's income, the wife's income, and nonlabor income.

3. The husband's (wife's) income refers to the median annual wage or salary income of full time year-round male (female) workers.[c]
4. The nonlabor income in a family constitutes additional income received by the family such as dividends, interest, and other miscellaneous income derived from property and financial transactions.
5. A husband's low income is associated with the high labor force participation rate of a married woman with husband present.
6. A low nonlabor income is associated with the high labor force participation rate of a married woman with husband present.
7. A wife's high income is associated with the high labor force participation rate of a married woman with husband present.

The linear equation was estimated, using the following form or its variation:

$$L = b_0 + b_1 Y_h + b_2 Y_w + b_3 Y_n + b_4 E + b_5 U_m + b_6 CC + v$$

where L	=	the labor force participation rate of married women with husband present during the census week (in percent);
$Y_h(Y_w)$	=	the medial annual wage or salary income of male (female) workers who worked 50-52 weeks in the year preceding the census;
$Y_h'(Y_w')$	=	the median annual wage or salary income of male (female) workers without other income;
Y_n	=	the mean nonlabor income other than wages and salary earnings and earnings from self employment;
Y_n'	=	the median annual wage or salary income of all workers with other income minus the median annual wage or salary income of all workers without other income;
E	=	median years of schooling completed by females 25 years and older;
U_m	=	the male unemployment rate;
CC	=	the cost of day care per child under 6 years of age per week;
C	=	the proportion of families who have one or more children under 6 years of age;
C_1	=	the number of children under 5 years of age per 1,000 women 15 to 49 years old; and
v	=	the disturbance term.

[c]Many wives work part time and part year. It is realistic to the adjusted female labor income for differences in employment status. But in the absence of such data for each SMSA no such attempt was made in this study.

A summary of results is presented in Table C-1. The table indicates that a husband's low income is associated with the high labor force participation rate of a married woman. In 1970, for example, the regression coefficient of Y_h (−.38) in Table C-1 provides a measure of the marginal rate of decrease in the labor force participation rate of the wife as the husband's income rises. The regression coefficient of nonlabor income (−.13) is interpreted in the same way as the husband's income. On the other hand, a wife's high income is associated with her high participation rate in the labor force. The regression coefficient of Y_w (.46) measures the marginal rate of increase in the labor force participation rate of the wife. High educational attainment is also associated with the high labor force participation rate of the wife. The marginal rate of increase in the labor force participation of the wife is 1.00 as educational attainment rises. High male unemployment is associated with the low labor force participation of the wife. The marginal rate of decrease in the labor force participation of the wife is −1.59 as the male unemployment rate rises. A high cost of child care is associated with the low labor force participation rate of the wife. The marginal rate of decrease in the labor force participation is (−.46) as the cost of child care rises.

Forty-four percent of the dependent variable was explained by six independent variables. Each of the six independent variables was statistically significant at the 5 percent level.

For comparability of regression coefficients in arithmetic form with those in logarithmic form compute the elasticity estimate in each of the six regression coefficients for the supply of married women. Elasticity estimate is defined as the regression coefficient of X in arithmetic form, b, multiplied by the ratio of the average of X to the average of Y where $X(Y)$ is the independent (dependent) variable.

Nonlabor Income

As mentioned earlier, nonlabor income has an income effect on the labor force participation of the wife. We should then expect that the regression coefficient of nonlabor income should be similar in size to that of the husband's income.

To handle this problem, we test the null hypothesis that the regression coefficient of nonlabor income is not significantly different from that of the husband's income. Results indicate that the null hypothesis is not rejected at the 5 percent level.

Income and Substitution Effects

The theoretical approach we take is that of Cain and Cipriani. Our problem is

Table C-1
Regression Results: Supply of Married Women, Single Women; and Demand for Women, SMSAs, 1940-70 (*t* values in parentheses)

Independent Variable	*1940*	*1950*	*1960*	*1970*	*1940*	*1950*	*1960*	*1970*
				Supply of Married Women				
	Arithmetic form				*Logarithmic form*			
Y_w		2.29 (3.80)	1.07 (3.24)	.46 (4.34)		1.95 (3.53)	1.22 (3.13)	.52 (4.48)
Y'_w	1.25 (1.15)				.03 (.07)			
Y_h		−1.53 (3.97)	− .86 (4.58)	− .22 (4.35)		−1.89 (3.62)	−1.32 (4.12)	− .38 (4.06)
Y'_h	−1.85 (2.14)				− .57 (.85)			
Y_n		− .75 (1.35)	− .97 (2.53)	− .13 (2.11)		− .16 (.98)	− .13 (1.98)	− .10 (2.44)
E	.54 (.81)	.95 (1.88)	1.16 (2.74)	1.00 (2.01)	.29 (.62)	.45 (1.82)	.35 (2.21)	.29 (1.01)
U_m	− .72 (3.26)	−1.04 (4.49)	−1.10 (6.69)	−1.59 (5.90)	− .67 (2.33)	− .22 (4.33)	− .21 (6.03)	− .17 (6.71)
C		− .46 (1.36)				− .63 (3.00)		
C_1	− .70 (2.77)				− .94 (2.29)			
CC			−1.56 (1.79)	− .46 (.30)			− .46 (1.02)	− .19 (.23)
Constant	48.69	38.07	46.02	35.79	8.00	5.58	4.97	3.31
R^2	.48	.48	.51	.44	.21	.23	.20	.39

	Supply of Single Women				Supply of Other Single Women			
	Arithmetic form				*Arithmetic form*			
Y_w		.20 (.78)	.50 (3.25)	.67 (6.71)		.44 (1.74)	– .07 (.81)	.19 (1.88)
Y'_w	1.35 (7.55)				1.56 (8.37)			
E	.45 (1.84)	1.85 (4.88)	2.51 (1.71)	2.53 (1.73)	2.68 (9.90)	1.08 (2.84)	.81 (2.23)	2.60 (1.82)
U_m	– .11 (1.43)	– .94 (12.12)	– .97 (2.66)	–1.61 (4.17)	–1.34 (8.22)	–1.54 (19.72)	– .85 (5.60)	–1.00 (2.63)
Constant	65.53	51.28	52.84	50.01	53.27	26.35	26.26	4.60
R^2	.47	.50	.48	.45	.48	.47	.49	.40

Demand for Women

	Arithmetic form			*Logarithmic form*		
E	.81 (2.25)	.63 (1.10)	2.62 (3.25)	.26 (2.09)	.18 (1.23)	.73 (3.71)
U_m	– .36 (1.54)	–1.10 (3.97)	– .93 (3.92)	– .06 (1.48)	– .19 (5.29)	– .08 (3.44)
F	.32 (3.17)	.24 (1.19)	.24 (2.84)	.36 (3.72)	.17 (1.49)	.26 (3.12)
Constant	15.20	28.63	5.30	1.69	2.87	1.06
R^2	.26	.21	.23	.27	.30	.23

Sources: See Appendix D.

how to separate the substitution effect from the income effect. Consider that a wife is engaged in unpaid household work, but she is now interested in market work outside the home. She gives second thoughts to the question of participating in the labor force. She asks herself whether it is worthwhile to work outside the home, giving up eight or more hours at home. To understand her problem, we must separate the economic value of household work into two parts: (1) the amount which it would cost her to employ a substitute to perform her household work; and (2) the satisfaction derived by her from performing the work. The problem becomes as follows. Her unpaid household work consists of the first category of measurable return, which we call compensated household work; the second category of satisfaction unmeasurable by the market, we call uncompensated home work. She would not attach economic value to the uncompensated household work, according to Kosters.[6] If the economic value of compensated household work is greater than market work, she would not prefer market work to household work. If, however, the economic value of compensated household work were less than market work, she would tend to work outside the home. It is this measurable economic value of household work that plays a role in determining whether the wife works outside the home or not. It is, therefore, necessary and meaningful, Kosters insists, to separate the economic value of household work, that is, compensated household work from uncompensated household work. Referring to the substitution and income effects it is assumed that the compensated household work gives the woman a pure substitution effect and the uncompensated household work gives her an income effect. Thus, the pure substitution effect indicates a shift from household work to market work. In symbols we write the regression equation in logarithmic form

$$\log L = b_1 \log Y_w + \log v$$

where b_1 is the elasticity estimate of L with respect to Y_w. It is b_1 that contains both the elasticity of compensated household work with respect to Y_w and the elasticity of uncompensated home work with respect to Y_w. Our problem is, then, to separate b_1 into two elasticities, i.e., the pure substitution elasticity of L with respect to Y_w, and the income elasticity of L with respect to Y_w.

Let us now translate what we have discussed into two equations (C-1) and (C-2).

$$L = a_1 Y_w + a_2 Y_h + a_3 Y_n + (a_4 Y_w) + v_1 \qquad \text{(C-1)}$$

$$L = b_1 Y_w + b_2 Y_h + b_3 Y_n + v_2 \qquad \text{(C-2)}$$

where $b_1 = a_1 + a_4$;

$b_2 = a_2$;

$b_3 = a_3$; and

ν_1, ν_2 = the disturbance terms in Equations (C-1) and (C-2).

Equation (C-1) provides a theoretical interpretation of Equation (C-2). Simply stated, the observed regression coefficient of the wife's income (b_1) is the sum of an income effect (a_4) and a pure substitution effect (a_1). The relationship between the observed substitution elasticity (b_1) and the pure substitution elasticity (b_1^*) is written as

$$b_1 = b_1^* + b_3 \left(\frac{\bar{Y}_w}{\bar{Y}_n} \right) \qquad \text{(C-3)}^{d}$$

where b_1 = the observed substitution elasticity of L with respect to Y_w ;

b_1^* = the pure substitution elasticity of L with respect to Y_w;

b_3 = the income elasticity of L with respect to Y_n;

$\bar{Y}_w$ = the average of Y_w; and

$\bar{Y}_n$ = the average of Y_n.

The pure substitution elasticity derived from Equation (C-3) does not, however, indicate whether it is underestimated or overestimated. Thus, it is necessary to provide another measure of the pure substitution elasticity to indicate the magnitude of another pure substitution elasticity. Cain provides another measure of the pure substitution elasticity.[e] That is,

$$b_1 = b_1^* + b_2 \left(\frac{\bar{Y}_w}{\bar{Y}_h} \right) \qquad \text{(C-4)}$$

where b_2 = the income elasticity of L with respect to Y_h; and

$\bar{Y}_h$ = the average of Y_n.

Applying Equations (C-3) and (C-4) to regression results for married women gives the following results: that b_1^* based on Equation (C-3) is 2.43, 2.20, and .76 in 1950, 1960, and 1970 respectively while b_1^* based on Equation (C-4) is 3.16, 2.03, and .60 in 1950, 1960, and 1970 respectively.[f]

---

[d]For a detailed discussion of this equation see Cain, *op. cit.*, pp. 10-13.

[e]For a detailed discussion of Equations (C-3) and (C-4) used in this section see Cain, *op. cit.*, pp. 8-13.

[f]For 1960 $\bar{Y}_w/\bar{Y}_n$ = \$3204/\$427 = 7.57 and $\bar{Y}_w/\bar{Y}_h$ = \$3204/\$5219 = .61. b_1, b_2, and b_3 are 1.22, –1.32, and –.13 respectively.

Both Equations (C-3) and (C-4) indicate that nonlabor income is assumed to be a proxy of the wife's uncompensated home work. Results show that the elasticity of pure substitution is greater than the observed substitution elasticity for 1950 to 1970. This appears to confirm Mincer's hypothesis (when the substitution effect is greater than the income effect, the long-term increase in participation of women in the labor force can be explained). However, this interpretation cannot be justified because the income elasticity attributable to nonlabor income is completely ignored.

We now obtain the net effect of income and substitution elasticities on the labor force participation rate of married women with husband present. The net effect is defined as the difference between pure substitution elasticity and combined income elasticities (sum of elasticities of the labor force participation rate of married women with husband present with respect to part of wife's income, husband's income and nonlabor income) was −.10, −.23, and −.04 for 1950, 1960, and 1970 respectively.[g]

This indicates that Mincer's hypothesis is not supported. Thus, we conclude that an explanation for the rise in the labor force participation of married women with husband present must be found in factors other than the husband's income, the wife's income, and nonlabor income while recognizing the importance of these income variables.

Educational Attainment

Educational attainment was found to be the key variable in our results. This variable was statistically significant at the five percent level in 1940, 1950, 1960, and 1970. The increase in educational attainment is positively associated with the increase in the labor force participation rate of the wife.

According to one group of economists,[7] the more education one has, the higher one's economic return. However, whether this kind of economic interpretation of educational attainment is valid for married women with husband present requires further research. Behavioral psychology might be able to determine better whether education is a consumer good or an investment good.

For 1950 $\bar{Y}_w/\bar{Y}_n$ = \$2014/\$666 = 3.02 and $\bar{Y}_w/Y_h$ = \$2014/\$3105 = .64. b_1, b_2, and b_3 are 1.95, −1.89, and −.16 respectively.

For 1970 $\bar{Y}_w/\bar{Y}_n$ = \$6199/\$2695 = .23 and $\bar{Y}_w/\bar{Y}_h$ = \$6199/\$9598 = .64. b_1, b_2, and b_3 are .46, −.22 and −.13 respectively.

---

[g]Substitution elasticity, defined as elasticity of labor force participation rate of married women with respect to wife's income, includes both pure substitution elasticity and income elasticity. Substitution elasticity (1.95, 1.22, and .52) constitutes pure substitution elasticity (2.43, 2.20, and .76) and income elasticity (−.48, −.98, and −.24) for 1950, 1960, and 1970 respectively.

Unemployment Rates

Three rates of unemployment, the male unemployment rate, the female unemployment rate, and total unemployment rate, have been examined to determine whether each of the three rates of unemployment has a different effect on the participation of married women in the labor force. Without exception the three variables were negative in sign and were statistically significant for 1940, 1950, 1960, and 1970.

Mincer objects to the use of the male unemployment rate as a proxy of employment conditions because both the male and female labor force move in the same direction.[8] Mincer then suggests the variable, U_x/P_x where U_x is the number of male unemployed and P_x, male population. However, the use of the variable, U_x/P_x, as a proxy of employment conditions is not convincing. As indicated earlier, the female unemployment rate is correlated with the extent of the labor force participation of women. Therefore, it is not a valid measure as an independent variable in a regression seeking to explain the participation rate of women in the labor force.

The Cost of Child Care

This variable was found to be very important in affecting the labor force participation of married women with husband present. The only reservation we have to make is that data on the average cost of child care were derived from public child care facilities for 1960. Therefore, our estimate of the average cost of child care was underestimated. But estimates on the average cost of child care are based on private and public costs in 1970.

Supply of Single Women

Single women constitutes single women never married, and women who are separated, divorced, or married with husband absent. We denote the former "single women" and the latter "other single women." The labor force participation rate of single women was made a function of the female income, educational attainment, and the male unemployment. We assumed that single women received neither nonlabor income nor other income.

The linear equation was estimated, using the following form:

$$L_s(L_{0t}) = b_0 + b_1 Y_w + b_2 E + b_3 U_m + v$$

where L_s = the labor force participation rate of single women never married 25 to 64 years old;

L_{0t} = the labor force participation rate of single women of other marital status 25 to 64 years old;

Definitions of Y_w to v are the same as those on page 00.

The regression coefficients of Y_w, E, and U_m for "single women" and "other single women" are correct in sign and are statistically significant, except that the regression coefficients of Y_w for "other single women" in 1960 was negative in sign and was statistically insignificant.

The regression coefficients of Y_w for "single women" are smaller than those of Y_w for married women for 1950 and 1960 and not for 1970. An explanation for this would require further reserach. The data are not such that we can make the proper interpretation of the regression coefficient, Y_w, for "single women."

As for the effect of educational attainment on the labor force participation, it is interesting to note that the regression coefficient of E for "single women" is about twice as large as that of E for married women in 1950 and 1960, and one and one-half times as large as that of E in 1970. An explanation of this would require further research.

The effect of the male unemployment rate on the labor force participation of "single women" is negative for 1940, 1950, 1960, and 1970. As mentioned in the discussion of married women, the sign of regression coefficient of the male unemployment rate might also be interpreted as the discouraged worker hypothesis.

Nearly fifty percent of the variation of the dependent variable was explained by three independent variables, and the remaining 50 percent of the variation was still left unexplained.

Demand for Women

The demand for women, defined as the proportion of women in the work force, was made a function of three independent variables, educational attainment, the male unemployment rate, and the expected female employment share. The linear equation was estimated, using the following form

$$L_w = b_0 + b_1 E + b_2 U_m + b_3 F + v$$

where L_w = the LFPR of women.

Two positive factors affecting the demand for women were educational attainment and the expected female employment share. High educational attainment is associated with a high demand for women. The marginal rate of increase in the demand for women is 2.62 for 1970. The expected female employment share is also positively associated with the demand for women. The marginal rate of increase in the demand for women is .24 for 1970. The negative

sign of the male unemployment rate does appear to support the discouragement hypothesis which is in conformity with that of the supply equation, suggesting that the discouragement hypothesis may be interpreted as the reduced demand hypothesis in the demand equation.

Each of the three variables was statistically significant at the 5 percent level. About 40 percent of the variation of the dependent variable was explained by the three independent variables and the remaining 60 percent of the variation was still left unexplained.

Note 1
A Brief Description of the Variables Used in Regressions

The variables included in the 1960 data are comparable with those available in the 1940 and 1950 data. There are, however, differences in the definition of variables and in the comparability of variables. A brief discussion of these variables is presented below:

1. The husband's (the wife's) income is the median annual wage or salary income of full time year-round male (female) workers in 1950 and 1960, but is the median annual wage or salary income of full time and part time male (female) workers in 1940.

2. In 1960 nonlabor income was obtained on the basis of the aggregate amount of nonlabor income (all kinds of aggregate income minus aggregate wage and salary income minus aggregate income of the self-employed) divided by all income recipients in the SMSA who received any kind of income. In 1950 nonlabor income was computed on the basis of the median nonlabor income per adult recipient in the SMA who received earnings other than wage and salary earnings and earnings from self employment. The average nonlabor income in 1950 was $666 compared with $423 in 1960 because nonlabor income in 1960 was spread over all income recipients, adults and nonadults. Of the two, the 1950 measure of nonlabor income is preferred to the 1960 measure of nonlabor income. Nonlabor income in 1940 is the median wage or salary income of all workers with other income minus the median wage or salary income of all workers without other income. This is a poor variable in concept compared with nonlabor income for 1950. Nonlabor income in some cities was even negative. This was because the median income with other income was smaller than the median income with no other income.

3. As will be discussed in Note 2 of Appendix C, the cost of child care was computed in 1960. In the absence of such data for 1940 and 1950, however, we employed alternative variables, the proportion of families who have one child or more under 6 years of age for 1950 and the number of children under 5 years of age per 1,000 women 15 to 49 years old for 1940.

4. Other variables included in regressions are comparable. These are the male unemployment rate, educational attainment, the expected female employment share, and the income of women as a percentage of the income of men.

Note 2
Estimate of the Cost of Child Care

First, we compute the weighted average cost of day care per child under 6 years of age for the United States. In symbols we write

$$C = p_i c_i$$

where C = the weighted average cost of day care per child under 6 years of age for the United States;

p_i = the proportion of families who have children under 6 years of age and whose child care cost falls in the ith group; and

c_i = the average amount paid per week falling in the ith group.

There are three groups, the first group pays under \$5, the second between \$5 and \$9, and the third \$10 or more. A midpoint is assumed to represent the average cost for each group. For the third group \$12 is assumed as a midpoint.

Second, C thus obtained is adjusted for differences in the average child care cost attributable to the difference in the family income by setting the average child care cost for the average family income for the United States equal to 100.

Third, the adjusted child care cost thus obtained is further adjusted for differences in the average child care cost attributable to the difference in region. Final results are:[9]

Region	*Average Cost*
North East	\$6.62
North Central	6.51
South	6.24
West	6.85
United States	6.55

Note 3
Estimate of the Expected Female Employment Share

First, we compute the female employment share of the ith occupational group for the United States. In symbols we write

$$r_i = \left(\frac{F}{M+F}\right)_i = \left(\frac{F}{T}\right)_i$$

where F = the number of female workers in the ith occupational group;

M = the number of male workers in the ith occupational group; and

T = $F + M$.

Second, we compute the expected female employment share of the ith occupational group in the jth SMSA. This can be done by multiplying r_i by all male and female employed workers of the ith occupation in the jth SMSA. This indicates that the female employment share of the ith occupation for the United States is expected to be the same for each SMSA. In symbols we write

$$F_{ij} = (T_{ij})r_i$$

where T_{ij} = all male and female workers in the ith occupational group in the jth SMSA; and

F_{ij} = the expected female employment share in the ith occupational group in the jth SMSA.

Finally, we compute the expected female employment share for the jth SMSA by summing F_{ij} for $i = 1, 2, \ldots n$ and dividing F_{ij} by T_j. In symbols we write

$$F_j = \frac{F_{ij}}{T_j}$$

where F_j = the expected female employment share for the jth SMSA; and

T_j = all male and female employed workers in the jth SMSA.

Appendix D
Sources, Means, and Standard Deviations of Variables Used in Chapter 6 with Census Data

Table D-1
Sources, Means, and Standard Deviations of Variables Used in Regressions with Census Data in Chapter 6

Variable	*Year*	*Mean*	*Standard Deviation*	*Source*
L	1940	17.08	4.62	PC(3), 11 & 12[a]
	1950	22.89	4.02	PC(2)1, 183
	1960	31.39	3.88	PC(1)C2-51, 33
	1970	40.14	4.48	PC(1)C2-51, 41
L_s	1940	72.93	4.07	PC(3), 11 & 12[a]
	1950	69.43	6.25	PC(2)1, 183
	1960	68.09	5.87	PC(1)D2-51, 116
	1970	50.95	7.01	PC(1)D2-51, 165
L_{0t}	1940	51.02	6.39	PC(3), 11 and 12[a]
	1950	51.19	6.53	PC(2)1, 183
	1960	50.01	6.91	PC(1)D2-51, 116
	1970	41.51	5.87	PC(1)D2-51, 165
L_w	1950	31.28	3.46	PC(2)1, 183
	1960	36.37	2.96	PC(1)D2-51, 116
	1970	42.37	3.85	PC(1)C2-51, 41
Y_w	1950	20.14	2.44	D11[b]
	1960	32.04	3.93	PC(1)D2-51, 136
	1970	61.99	9.42	PC(1)D2-51, 198
Y'_w	1940	7.00	1.62	PC(3), 12[c]
	1950	12.10	2.39	PC(2)1, 185
Y_h	1950	31.05	2.93	D11[b]
	1960	52.19	5.60	PC(1)D2-51, 135
	1970	95.98	12.21	PC(1)D2-51, 98
Y'_h	1940	11.82	1.86	PC(3), 12[c]
	1950	27.27	3.22	PC(2)1, 185
Y_{hw}	1970	122.90	12.01	PC(1)D2-51, 198
Y_n	1940	− .21	1.50	PC(3), 12[c]
	1950	6.66	.99	PC(2)2-51, 93
	1960	4.23	.90	PC(1)D2-51, 76[d]
	1970	26.95	5.78	PC(1)D2-51, 198[e]
E	1940	9.04	1.00	PC(2)1, 60
	1950	10.30	1.07	PC(2)2-49, 65
	1960	11.16	.84	PC(1)C2-51, 73
	1970	12.02	2.40	PC(1)C2-51, 83

Table D-1 continued

Variable	*Year*	*Mean*	*Standard Deviation*	*Source*
U_m	1940	11.69	2.65	PC(2)1, 66
	1950	5.28	1.75	PC(2)1, 89
	1960	5.18	1.91	PC(1)D2-51, 115
	1970	3.75	1.39	PC(1)D2-51, 164
U_f	1940	10.73	2.31	PC(2)1, 67
	1950	4.63	1.71	PC(2)1, 89
	1960	5.31	1.66	PC(1)D2-51, 115
	1970	5.21	1.54	PC(1)D2-51, 164
CC	1960	6.55	.22	A46, 47, & M24[f]
	1970	2.41	.25	9[g]
C	1950	29.35	2.56	PC(4)2A, 40
	1960	32.21	3.93	PC(1)C2-51, 32
	1970	26.73	2.75	PC(1)C2-51, 41
C'	1940	21.27	2.30	37[h]
	1950	16.34	17.58	37[h]
F	1940	29.33	4.64	PC(3)1, 58 & PC(3)2-5, 11
	1950	30.48	4.17	PC(2)1, 125 & 73[h]
	1960	27.56	2.66	PC(1)D2-51, 121
	1970	38.45	3.78	PC(1)D2-51, 171

Note: PC(3), 11 & 12 stands for Census of Population, Vol. 3, Tables 11 and 12.

[a]Refers to Employment and Family Characteristics of Women of Volume 3.

[b]Gertrude Bancroft, *The American Labor Force* (New York: Wiley, 1959).

[c]Refers to Wage and Salary Income in 1949 of Volume 3.

[d]Figures are based on Table 76 of the 1960 Census of Population, Vol. 1, Parts 2-51.

$$Y_n = \frac{YT - Y_1T_1 - Y_2T_2}{T}$$

where Y_n = nonlabor income; T = all income recipients; Y = mean income of all income recipients; Y_1 = mean income of wage & salary income recipients; T_1 = number of wage or salary income recipients; T_2 = the number of self employed.

[e]In 1970 $Y_n = Y_{hw} - Y_h$ where Y_{hw} = median income of husband-wife families (both employed); and Y_h = median income of one worker families (husband employed and wife not working).

[f]Department of Health, Education and Welfare, *Child Care Arrangements of Working Mothers in the United States,* Tables A-46, A-47, and M-24; and *Time Lost from Work Among the Currently Employed Population. United States 1968,* Table 9.

[g]*Ibid.*

[h]W. H. Graybill et al., *The Fertility of American Women* (New York: Wiley, 1958).

Notes

Chapter 1
Introduction

1. William H. Chafe, *The American Woman* (New York: Oxford University Press, 1972), pp. 237-42.

2. Gary Becker, *The Economics of Discrimination* (Chicago: University of Chicago, 1957); Lester Thurow, *Poverty and Discrimination* (Washington, D.C.: Brookings Institution, 1969); Malcolm Cohen, "Sex Differences in Compensation." *Journal of Human Resources,* Vol. 6 (Fall, 1971); James Gwartney, "Discrimination and Income Differentials," *American Economic Review,* Vol. 60 (June, 1970); Barbara Bergmann, "The Effect on White Incomes of Discrimination," *Journal of Political Economy,* Vol. 79 (March-April, 1971); Kenneth Arrow, "Some Models of Racial Discrimination," (Mimeographed); Lloyd Atkinson, "Occupation and Income Projections, 1969-1975," (Mimeographed).

3. Cynthia Epstein, "Encountering the Male Establishment: Sex-Status Limits on Women's Careers in the Professions," *American Journal of Sociology,* Vol. 75 (May, 1970); Michael P. Fogarty et al. *Sex, Career and Family* (London: George Allen and Unwin, 1971); R. Ishwaran, ed., *Family Issues of Employed Women in Europe and America* (Leiden: Brill, 1971); Rhona and Robert Rapopport, *Dual-Career Families* (London: Penguin Books, 1971).

4. Jacob Mincer, "Labor Force Participation of Married Women," in *Aspects of Labor Economics,* Universities-National Bureau Committee for Economic Research (Princeton: Princeton University Press, 1962); Glen Cain, *Married Women in the Labor Force* (Chicago: University of Chicago, 1964); William Bowen and T. Finegan, *The Economics of Labor Force Participation* (Princeton: Princeton University Press, 1969); Corindo Cipriani, *A Labor Market Model: Married Women* (Ph.D. Dissertation, University of Minnesota, 1970).

Chapter 2
Trends in Total Discrimination

1. For a fuller discussion see Sheila Tobias and Lisa Anderson. "What Ever Happened to Rosie the Riveter?" *MS.*, Vol. 1, No. 12 (June, 1973), pp. 92-98.

Chapter 3
Components of Discrimination

1. S.C. Travis, "The U.S. Labor Force: Projection to 1985," in *Monthly Labor Review,* Vol. 90 (May, 1970).

2. Bureau of the Census, *1950 Census of Population,* Vol. 4, Part 7-A, Table 28.

3. National Educational Association, *Research Report,* 1966R6.

4. Bureau of the Census, *op. cit.*

5. U.S. Civil Service Commission, *Study of Women Employees,* 1968.

Chapter 4
Factors Affecting Income Discrimination

1. Bureau of Labor Statistics, *Comparative Job Performance by Age: Office Work* (Bulletin 1273, 1960); and *Comparative Job Performance by Age: Large Plants in 16 Men's Footwear and Household Furniture Industries* (Bulletin 1223, 1952).

2. Jessie Bernard, *Academic Women,* (University Park, Pennsylvania State University, 1964), pp. 263-69.

3. Radcliffe College, *Graduate Education for Women: The Radcliffe Ph.Ds.* (Cambridge: Harvard University Press, 1956), p. 51.

4. Gwartney, *op. cit.*

5. John Buckley, "Pay Differences Between Men and Women in the Same Job," in *Monthly Labor Review,* Vol. 94 (November, 1971).

6. Edward J. O'Boyle, "Job Tenure: How It Relates to Race and Age," in *Monthly Labor Review,* Vol. 92 (September, 1969), p. 16.

7. E. Lanham and L.B. Dawkins, *Women in Business: Equal Pay for Equal Work,* Bureau of Business Research, University of Texas, 1959, p. 14.

8. Bureau of Labor Statistics, "Labor Turnover of Women Factory Workers 1950-55," in *Monthly Labor Review,* Vol. 78 (August, 1955), p. 889.

9. Women's Bureau, *Facts About Women's Absenteeism* (1969), p. 2.

10. John Parrish, "Employment of Women Chemists in Industrial Laboratories," in *Science,* Vol. 148 (April 30, 1965), pp. 657-8.

11. Gary S. Becker, *Investment in Human Capital,* (New York, Columbia University Press, 1964) and W.Y. Li, "Labor as a Quasi-Fixed Factor," in *Journal of Political Economy,* Vol. 70 (December, 1962), pp. 538-555.

12. American Management Association, *Supervisory Management Letter* No. 3, 1958.

13. Women's Bureau, *Day Care Service: Industry's Involvement* (Bulletin 296, 1971), p. 23.

14. *Ibid.*

15. *Ibid.*

16. *Ibid.*

17. D.G. Johnson and E.B. Hutchings, "Doctor or Dropout?: A Study of Medical Student Attrition," in *Journal of Medical Education,* Vol. 41 (December, 1966), p. 1140.

18. *Ibid.*

19. *Code of Federal Regulations,* Title 29, Part 800.119 (Revised as of January 1, 1971).

20. *Ibid.,* Part 800.125.

21. *Ibid.,* Part 800.127.

22. *Ibid.,* Part 800.129

23. *Ibid.,* Part 800.131.

24. 421 F. 2d 263 (1967).

25. T.E. Murphy, "Female Wage Discrimination: A Study of the Equal Pay Act," in *University of Cincinatti Law Review,* Vol. 39 (fall, 1970), p. 623.

Chapter 5
Factors Affecting Occupational Discrimination

1. Edward W. Noland and Edward W. Bakke, *Workers Wanted: A Study of Employers Hiring Policies, Preferences, and Practices in New Haven and Charlotte* (New York: Harper, 1949).

2. National Manpower Council, *Woman Power* (New York: Columbia University Press, 1957).

3. Charles E. Grindler, *Office Executive,* Vol. 36 (January, 1961), pp. 10-13.

4. U.S. Department of Labor, Manpower Administration, *Dual Career,* Vol. 1 (Washington, D.C.: Government Printing Office, 1970).

5. Eleanor Schwartz, *The Sex Barrier in Business* (Atlanta: Georgia State University, 1971), p. 71.

6. Douglas C. Basil, *Women in Management: Performance, Prejudice, and Promotion* (New York: Dunellen, 1972).

7. Cynthia F. Epstein, "Encountering the Male Establishment: Sex Status Limits on Women's Careers in the Professions," in *American Journal of Sociology,* Vol. 75 (May, 1970).

8. Jessie Bernard, *Academic Women* (University Park: Pennsylvania State University Press, 1964).

9. Rita J. Simon and Evelyn Rosenthal, "Profile of the Woman Ph.D. in Economics, History, and Sociology," *Association of American University Women Journal,* Vol. 60 (March, 1967), pp. 127-129.

10. Michael P. Fogarty et al., *Sex, Career and Family* (London: George Allen and Unwin, 1971) p. 135 and pp. 432-448.

11. *Ibid.,* p. 505.

12. *Ibid.,* p. 47.

13. Eleanor Maccoby, "Sex Difference in Intellectual Functioning," in *The Development of Sex Differences,* E. Maccoby, ed., (Stanford: Stanford University Press, 1966), pp. 25-55.

14. Jerome Kagan and others, "The Psychological Significance of Styles of Conceptualization," in *Basic Cognitive Processes in Children,* J.C. Wright and J. Kagan, eds., Monograph no. 86, Social Research Child Development, 1963.

15. James Pierce, "Sex Differences in Achievement and Motivation of Able High School Students," in *Co-Operative Research Project* No. 1097, University of Chicago, December, 1961.

16. M.S. Horner, "Women's Will to Fail," *Psychology Today,* Vol. 3, No. 6 (November, 1969), p. 36.

17. Naomi Weisstein, "Kinder Kuche, Kirche, As Scientific Law: Psychology Constructs the Female, " in *Discrimination Against Women,* Hearings before the Committee on Education and Labor, House of Representatives, 91st Congress, 2nd Session, Part 1, p. 291.

18. Norton T. Dodge, *Women in the Soviet Economy* (Baltimore: Johns Hopkins Press, 1966).

19. Bureau of Labor Statistics, *Special Labor Force Report,* No. 119.

20. Alice S. Rossi, *Academic Women on the Move* (New York: Russel Sage Foundation, 1973), p. 513.

21. *Ibid.,* pp. 511-512.

22. Maria Gutberger, "Services Designed to Help Women to Combine Occupational and Family Responsibilities," in *Employment of Women,* (Paris: OECD, 1970), pp. 229-237; Viola Klein, "Syncronization and Harmonization of Working Hours with the Openings and Closing of Social Services, Administrative Offices, etc.," *op. cit.,* pp. 239-253.

23. Rhona and Robert Rapopport, *Dual-Career Families* (London: Penguin Books, 1971), pp. 302-317.

24. Association of American Colleges, *Newsletters,* April through June, 1973.

Chapter 6
Factors Affecting Participation Discrimination

1. John D. Durand, *The Labor Force in the United States 1890-1960* (New York: Social Science Research Council, 1948), p. 59.

2. Seymour L. Wolfbein and A.I. Jaffe, "Demographic Factors in Labor Force Growth," in *Demographic Analysis,* J.J. Spengler and O.D. Duncan, eds., (New York: Free Press, 1956), pp. 492-96.

3. Stanley Lebergott, "Population Changes and the Supply of Labor," in *Demographic and Economic Changes in Developed Countries* (Princeton: Princeton University Press, 1960), p. 494.

4. V.K. Oppenheimer, *The Female Labor Force in the United States* (Berkeley: University of California, 1970), p. 26.

5. Robert Rapopport, "Dual-Career Families," in *Family Issues of Employed Women in Europe and America,* R. Ishwaran, ed., (Leiden: Brill, 1971).

6. Siegried Giedion, *Mechanization Takes Command* (New York: Oxford University Press, 1948), Part VI.

7. Clarence Long, *The Labor Force Under Changing Income and Employment* (Princeton: Princeton University Press, 1958), p. 120.

8. Bureau of the Census, *1960 Census of Population,* Vol. 2, Part 4-A, Tables 42 and 43.

9. Robert Smuts, *Women and Work in America* (New York: Columbia University Press, 1959).

10. Hadley Cantril, ed., *Public Opinion 1935-46* (Princeton: Princeton University Press, 1951), pp. 1044-48.

11. *Ibid.*

12. *Ibid.*

13. *Ibid.*

14. *Ibid.*

15. *Ibid.*

16. James N. Morgan et al., *Income and Welfare in the United States* (New York: McGraw Hill, 1962), pp. 112-113.

17. United States Department of Labor, Manpower Administration, *Dual Careers,* Vol. 1 (Government Printing Office, 1970), Table 3.26.

18. American Institute of Public Opinion, *Gallup Poll Index,* No. 63 (September, 1970).

19. Bureau of Labor Statistics, *Special Labor Force Report,* No. 103, Table 4.

Chapter 7
Summary and Conclusions

1. See quotations from the Swedish Institute Study, *Sweden Today: The Status of Women in Sweden,* a report to the United Nations in 1968, in Marjorie Galenson, *Women and Work: An International Comparison* (Ithaca: New York

State School of Industrial and Labor Relations, Cornell University, 1973), pp. 60-61.

Appendix C
Regression Analysis: The Supply of Married Women, Single Women; The Demand for Women

1. Jacob Mincer, "Labor Force Participation of Married Women," in *Aspects of Labor Economics* (Princeton: Princeton University Press, 1962).

2. Glen Cain, *Married Women in the Labor Force* (Chicago: University of Chicago Press, 1962); W.G. Bowen and T.A. Finegan, *The Economics of Labor Force Participation* (Princeton: Princeton University Press, 1969); Corindo Cipriani, *A Labor Market Model: Married Women* (Ph.D. Dissertation, University of Minnesota, 1970).

3. Durand, *op. cit.,* pp. 116-117.

4. Cain, *op. cit.,* p. 56.

5. Bowen and Finegan, *op. cit.,* pp. 772-776.

6. Marvin Kosters, *Income and Substitution Parameters in a Family Labor Supply Model* (Ph.D. Dissertation, University of Chicago, 1966).

7. Gary S. Becker, "Investment in Human Capital: A Theoretical Analysis," *Journal of Political Economy,* Vol. 70 (October, 1962 Supplement), pp. 9-50; W.G. Bowen, *Economic Aspects of Education* (Princeton: Princeton University Press, 1964), pp. 3-41; M. Blaug, "The Rate of Return on Investment in Education in Great Britain," *Manchester School,* Vol. 36 (September, 1965), pp. 205-62; M. Blaug, *Economics of Education: A Selected Annotated Bibliography* (New York: Pergamon Press, 1968), p. 15.

8. Jacob Mincer, "Labor Force Participation and Unemployment," in *Prosperity and Unemployment,* R.A. Gordon and M.S. Gordon, eds., (Berkeley: University of California Press, 1966), p. 79.

9. Department of Health, Education and Welfare, *Child Care Arrangements of Working Mothers in the United States* (Children's Bureau Publication No. 461), Tables A-45, A-47, and M-24.

Selected Bibliography

Public Documents

U.S. Bureau of the Census. *Historical Statistics of the United States: Colonial Time to 1957; Historical Statistics of the United States: Continuation to 1962 and Revisions; Occupational Trends in the United States 1900-1950; 1940 Census of Population,* Vols. 2 and 3; *1950 Census of Population,* Vols. 2 and 4; *1960 Census of Population,* Vol. 1; *1970 Census of Housing* (Advanced Report); *1970 Census of Population,* Vols. 1 and 2; *Statistical Abstracts of the United States* 1970 and 1971; *Current Population Report,* P-20 and P-60.

U.S. Bureau of Labor Statistics. *Comparative Job Performance by Age: Large Plants in the Men's Footwear and Household Furniture Industries* (Bulletin 1223, 1952); *Comparative Job Performance by Age: Office Workers* (Bulletin 1273, 1960); *College Educated Workers 1968-80* (Bulletin 1676, 1970); and *Special Labor Force Report.*

U.S. Civil Service Commission. *Study of Employment of Women in the Federal Government* 1968 (June, 1969).

U.S. *Code of Federal Regulations,* Title 29, Part 800 (January, 1971).

U.S. *Fair Employment Practices,* EEOC Decisions (Washington, D.C.: Commerce Clearing House).

U.S. *Federal Reporter,* 2nd Series, Vols. 420, 421, and 424.

U.S. *Federal Supplement,* Vols. 265 and 288 (St. Paul: West Publishing Company).

U.S. Department of Health, Education and Welfare. *Selected Health Characteristics by Occupation: U.S., July 1961-June 1963* (Publication No. 1000, Series 10, No. 21); *Child Care Arrangements of Working Mothers in the U.S.* (Publication No. 461); *Time Lost from Work Among the Currently Employed Population, 1968.*

U.S. House of Representatives. *Discrimination Against Women* Hearings before the Special Subcommittee on Education of the Committee on Education and Labor, 91st Congress, 2nd Session, Parts 1 and 2 (1970).

U.S. Manpower Administration. *Dual Careers,* Vol. 1 (Washington, D.C.: Government Printing Office, 1970).

U.S. National Archives. *Federal Register,* Vols. 30 and 33.

U.S. *Public Law,* Title 7, Chapter 88.

U.S. Women's Bureau. *The New Position of Women in American Industry* (Bulletin 12, 1920); *Case Studies in Equal Pay for Women* (Special Report D-16, September, 1951); *1969 Handbook on Women Workers* (Bulletin 294,

1969); *Facts About Women's Absenteeism* (1969); *Child Care Services Provided by Hospitals* (Bulletin 295, 1970); *Day Care Services: Industry's Involvement* (Bulletin 296, 1971).

Books

Astin, Helen S. *The Woman Doctorate in America* (New York: Russel Sage Foundation, 1969).

Becker, Gary S. *Investment in Human Capital* (New York: Columbia University Press, 1964).

Bernard, Jessi. *Academic Women* (University Park: Pennsylvania State University Press, 1964).

Blau, M. *Economics of Education: A Selected Annotated Bibliography* (New York: Pergamon Press, 1968).

Bowen, W.G. *Economic Aspects of Education* (Princeton: Princeton University Press, 1964).

Bowen, W.G. and Finegan, T.A. *The Economics of Labor Force Participation* (Princeton: Princeton University Press, 1969).

Cantril, Hadley. ed. *Public Opinion 1935-1946* (Princeton: Princeton University Press, 1969).

Chafe, William H. *The American Woman: Her Changing Social, Economic, and Political Roles 1920-70* (New York: Oxford University Press, 1972).

Dodge, Norton T. *Women in the Soviet Economy* (Baltimore: Johns Hopkins Press, 1966).

Durand, John. *The Labor Force in the United States, 1890-1960* (New York: Social Science Research Council, 1948).

Epstein, Cynthia F. *Women's Place* (Berkeley: University of California Press, 1970).

Fogarty, Michael et al. *Sex, Career and Family* (London: Allen and Unwin, 1971).

____. *Women in Top Jobs: Four Studies in Achievement* (London: Allen and Unwin, 1971).

Friedan, Betty. *The Feminine Mystique* (New York: Norton, 1963).

Galenson, Marjorie. *Women and Work: An International Comparison* (Ithaca: Labor Relations, Cornell University, 1973).

Giedion, Siegried. *Mechanization Takes Command* (New York: Oxford University Press, 1948).

Ginsberg, Eli and associates. *Life Style of Education Women* (New York: Columbia University Press, 1966).

Gordon, R.A. and Gordon, M.S. eds. *Prosperity and Unemployment* (Berkeley: University of California Press, 1966).

Kreps, Juanita. *Sex in the Market Place: American Women at Work* (Baltimore: Johns Hopkins Press, 1971).

Lebergott, Stanley. *Manpower in Economic Growth: The American Record Since 1800* (New York: McGraw Hill, 1964).

Lewis, H. Gregg. *Unionism and Relative Wages in the United States: An Empirical Inquiry* (Chicago: University of Chicago Press, 1963).

Lopate, Carol. *Women in Medicine* (Baltimore: Johns Hopkins Press, 1966).

Long, Clarence D. *The Labor Force Under Changing Income and Employment* (Princeton: Princeton University Press, 1958).

Mattfeld, J.A. and Van Aken, C.G. eds. *Women and the Scientific Professions* (Cambridge: M.I.T. Press, 1965).

Morgan, James et al. *Income and Welfare in the United States* (New York: McGraw Hill, 1962).

National Manpower Council. *Woman Power* (New York: Columbia University Press, 1957).

Noland, Edward W. and Bakke, Edward W. *Workers Wanted: A Study of Employers Hiring Policies, Preferences and Practices in New Haven and Charlotte* (New York: Harper, 1949).

Oppenheimer, V.K. *The Female Labor Force in the United States* (Berkeley: University of California Press, 1970).

Organization of Economic Cooperation and Development. *Employment of Women* (Paris: OECD, 1971).

Radcliffe College. *Graduate Education for Women: The Radcliffe Ph.Ds* (Cambridge: Harvard University Press, 1956).

Rapopport, Rhona and Robert. *Dual-Career Families* (London: Penguin Books, 1971).

Rossi, Alice S. et al. *Academic Women on the Move* (New York: Russel Sage Foundation, 1973).

Schwartz, Eleanor. *The Sex Barrier in Business* (Atlanta: Georgia State University, 1971).

Sibson, Robert E. *Wages and Salaries: A Handbook for Line Managers* (New York: American Management Association, 1967).

Seidman, Joel. *The Worker Views His Union* (Chicago: University of Chicago Press, 1958).

Smuts, Robert. *Women and Work in America* (New York: Columbia University Press, 1959).

Articles and Periodicals

Becker, Gray S. "Investment in Human Capital: A Theoretical Analysis," *Journal of Political Economy,* Vol. 70 (October, 1962 Supplement).

Blaug, M. "The Rate of Return on Investment in Education in Great Britain," *Manchester School of Economic and Social Studies,* Vol. 36 (September, 1965).

Blaug, Peter M. "Occupational Choice: A Conceptual Farmework," *Industrial Labor Relations Review,* Vol. 9 (1956).

Brown, Barbara A., Emerson, Thomas I., Falk, Gail and Freedman, Ann E. "The Equal Rights Amendment: A Constitutional Basis for Equal Rights for Women," *Yale Law Journal,* Vol. 5 (April, 1971), pp. 872-985.

Buckley, John. "Pay Differences Between Men and Women in the Same Job," *Monthly Labor Review,* Vol. 94 (November, 1971).

Cohen, Malcolm. "Sex Differences in Compensation," *Journal of Human Resources,* Vol. 6 (fall, 1971).

Dean, Burton V. et al. "Job Evaluation Upholds Discrimination Suit," *Industrial Engineering,* Vol. 3 (March, 1971).

Dinerman, D. "Sex Descrimination in the Legal Profession," in *Discrimination Against Women,* Hearings before the Special Subcommittee on Education and Labor, 91st Congress, 2d Session, Part 1 (1970).

Dykman, R.A. and Stalmaker, J.M. "Survey of Women Physicians Graduating from Medical School, 1925-1940," *Journal of Medical Education,* Vol. 32 (March, 1957).

Entwisle, George. "Medical Expenditures and Student Enrollment," *Journal of Medical Education,* Vol. 46 (February, 1971).

Epstein, Cynthia F. "Encountering the Male Establishment: Sex Status Limits on Women's Careers in the Professions," *American Journal of Sociology,* Vol. 75 (May, 1970).

Fisher, Ann and Golde, Peggy. "The Position of Women in Anthropology," *American Anthropologist,* Vol. 70 (April, 1968).

Fucks, Victor. "Differences in Hourly Earnings Between Men and Women," *Monthly Labor Review,* Vol. 74 (November, 1951).

Grinder, Charles E. "Factor of Sex in Office Management," *Office Executive,* Vol. 36 (February, 1961).

Gutburger, Maria. "Services Designed to Help Women to Combine Occupational and Family Responsibilities," in *Employment of Women,* Organization of Economic Cooperation and Development, Paris, 1971.

Horner, M.S. "Women's Will to Fail," *Psychology Today,* Vol. 3 (November, 1969).

Hutchings, E.S. "Minorities, Manpower, and Medicine," *Journal of Medical Education,* Vol. 46 (May, 1971).

Johnson, D.F. "Education of Adult Workers: Projections to 1985," *Monthly Labor Review,* Vol. 93 (August, 1970).

Johnson, D.G. and Hutchins, E.B. "Doctor or Dropout: A Study of Medical Student Attrition," *Journal of Medical Education,* Vol. 41 (December, 1966).

Kagan, Jerome et al. "The Psychological Significance of Styles of Conceptualization," *Basic Cognitive Processes in Children,* Wright, J.C. and Kagan, J. eds., (Monograph, Social Research Child Development 23, 1963).

Kaplan, H.I. "Studying Attitudes of the Medical Profession Toward Women Physicians: A Survey," in *Discrimination Against Women,* Hearings before the Special Subcommittee on Education and Labor, 91st Congress, 2d Session, Part 1 (1970).

Lamouse, Annette. "Family Roles of Women: A German Example," *Journal of Marriage and the Family,* Vol.31 (February, 1969).

Levitan, N. and Patinkin, D. "On the Economic Theory of Price Indexes," *Economic Development and Cultural Change,* Vol. 10 (April, 1961).

Maccoby, Eleanor. "Sex Differences in Intellectual Functioning," *Development of Sex Differences,* Maccoby, E. ed., (Stanford: Stanford University Press, 1966).

Michel, Andree. "Interaction and Goal Attainment in Parisian Working Wives' Families," *Family Issues of Employed Women in Europe and America,* Michel, Andree, ed., (Leiden: Brill, 1971).

Murphy, T.E. "Female Wage Discrimination: A Study of the Equal Pay Act," *University of Cincinnati Law Review,* Vol. 39 (fall, 1970).

National Education Association. *National Educational Assocation Research Report,* 1960-R3 and 1966-R2.

O'Boyle, Edward J. "Job Tenure: How It Relates to Race and Age," *Monthly Labor Review,* Vol. 92 (September, 1969).

Oi, W.Y. "Labor as a Quasi-Fixed Factor," *Journal of Political Economy,* Vol. 70 (December, 1962).

Parrish, John B. "Employment of Women Chemists in Industrial Laboratories," *Science,* Vol. 148 (April 30, 1965).

Pierce, James V. "Sex Difference in Achievement and Motivation of Able High School Students," Cooperative Research Project No. 1097, University of Chicago.

Piotrowski, Jerry. "The Employment of Married Women and the Changing Sex Roles in Poland," in *Family Issues of Employed Women in Europe and America,* Michel, Andree, ed., (Leiden: Brill, 1971).

Rossi, Alice S. "Job Discrimination and What Women Can Do About it?," in

Discrimination Against Women, Hearings before the Special Subcommittee on Education and Labor, 91st Congress, 2d Session, Part 1 (1970).

Rosenlund, M.L. and Oski, F.A. "Women in Medicine," *Annals of Internal Medicine,* Vol. 66 (1967).

Sandell, Steven H. "Discussion: What Economic Equality for Women Requires," *American Economic Review,* Vol. 62 (May, 1972).

Simon, Rita F. et al. "The Woman Ph.D.: A Recent Profile," *Social Problems,* Vol. 15 (fall, 1967).

Tobias, Sheila. "What Ever Happened to Rosie the Riveter?," *MS.,* Vol. 1, No. 12 (June, 1973).

Travis, S.C. "The U.S. Labor Force: Projection to 1985," *Monthly Labor Review,* Vol. 90 (May, 1970).

Weisstein, Naomi. "Kinder, Kuche, Kirche as Scientific Law: Psychology Constructs the Female," in *Discrimination Against Women,* Hearing before the Special Subcommittee on Education and Labor, 91st Congress, 2d Session, Part 1 (1970).

White, James. "Women in the Law," *Michigan Law Review,* Vol. 65 (April, 1967).

Woytinsky, W.S. "Additional Workers and the Volume of Unemployment in Depression," (New York: Social Science Research Council, 1940).

Zeller, Harriet. "Discrimination Against Women, Occupational Segregation, and the Relative Wages," *American Economic Review,* Vol. 62 (May, 1972).

Reports

American Institute of Public Opinion. *Gallup Poll Index,* No. 63 (September, 1970).

American Management Association. *Supervisory Management Letter,* No. 3, 1958.

American Economic Association. *The Structure of Economists Employment and Salaries in 1964* (A Supplement to *American Economic Review,* Vol. 55, December, 1965).

Association of American Colleges, *Newsletters,* April-June 1973.

Lanham, E. and Dawkins, L.B. *Women in Business: Equal Pay for Equal Work* (Bureau of Business Research, University of Texas, 1959).

National Science Foundation. *National Register of Scientific and Technical Personnel 1970 American Science Manpower 1970; Unemployment Rates and Employment Characteristics for Scientists and Engineers 1971.*

Unpublished Material

Cipriani, Corindo. *A Labor Market Model: Married Women* (Ph.D. Dissertation, University University of Minnesota, 1970).

Koster, Marvin. *Income and Substitution Parameters in a Family* (Ph.D. Dissertation, University of Chicago, 1966).

Sanborn, Henry N. *Income Differences Between Men and Women in the United States* (Ph.D. Dissertation, University of Chicago, 1960).

Sawhill, Isabel V. *Relative Gap in Earnings Between Men and Women in the United States* (Ph.D. Dissertation, New York University, 1968).

Index

Index

Tables are indicated by t, figures by f, and footnotes by n.

About the Authors

Robert Tsuchigane is an economist and consultant, specializing in the utilization of human resources. He taught at the State University of New York at Albany and, after receiving his doctorate at the University of Maryland, became assistant professor of economics at Maryland's Frostburg State College. Dr. Tsuchigane has participated in a number of research projects in the development and utilization of human resources.

Norton Dodge is an economist, specializing in the Soviet Union, and associate professor of economics at the University of Maryland. He graduated from Harvard University's Russian Regional Studies Program and was a graduate fellow at the Russian Research Center. Dr. Dodge is the author of *Women in the Soviet Economy: Their Roles in Economic, Scientific, and Technical Development* (Baltimore: The Johns Hopkins Press, 1966) and other studies on the Soviet economy and the role of women in economic development.